The Italian Executioners

The Italian Executioners

The Genocide of the Jews of Italy

SIMON LEVIS SULLAM

*Translated by Oona Smyth
with Claudia Patane*

With a foreword by David I. Kertzer

PRINCETON UNIVERSITY PRESS
PRINCETON & OXFORD

Requests for permission to reproduce material from this work should be sent to
Permissions, Princeton University Press

Published by Princeton University Press,
41 William Street, Princeton, New Jersey 08540

In the United Kingdom: Princeton University Press,
6 Oxford Street, Woodstock, Oxfordshire OX20 1TR

press.princeton.edu

Jacket art: Milan, Italy, 1943. SeM/Universal Images Group/Bridgeman Images

First published as *I carnefici italiani* in January 2015 by Giangiacomo Feltrinelli Editore, Milan, Italy. Copyright © 2015 Giangiacomo Feltrinelli Editore

ISBN 978-0-691-17905-6
Library of Congress Control Number 2018938054

British Library Cataloging-in-Publication Data is available

This book has been composed in Baskerville 120 Pro

Printed on acid-free paper. ∞

Printed in the United States of America

10 9 8 7 6 5 4 3 2 1

Contents

Foreword

The impulse to erase or recast painful historical memories may well be a universal human trait, but it can be a dangerous one. When the uncomfortable events of the past are replaced in memory—and, even worse, in historiography—by a triumphal account of virtue, the danger is all the greater. It is just such a misrepresentation of the past that Simon Levis Sullam tackles head-on in this short but important book.

Those who have spent much time in Italy in recent years may be pardoned if they get the impression that Italians fought in World War II not on the side of the Nazis but with the Americans and British against the Nazis. From the immediate postwar years to the present, memories of the relations between the Italians and the Nazis have focused for the most part on the Resistance. One small indication of this: Italy boasts dozens of centers for the study of the Resistance but few for the study of Fascism. Yet the Resistance lasted a year and a half and involved only limited parts of the country and a small minority of Italians. By contrast, the Fascist regime lasted two decades, covered the whole country, and involved millions.

If Italians are, understandably perhaps, eager to misremember their past support for the Fascist regime and their past alliance with Nazi Germany, they have shown themselves even more eager to construct a wholly

misleading history of their responsibility for the persecution and cold-blooded murder of their fellow Italians
whose only sin was being Jewish. It is this history that
Levis Sullam seeks to set straight in these pages.

In the widespread attempts to separate Italians from
any responsibility for the Holocaust, few elements have
been more central than ignoring Italy's vicious campaign
of persecution of its Jewish citizens that was launched
in 1938 with the introduction of the draconian racial
laws. Adults were thrown out of their jobs, their children
were thrown out of the schools, and all Jews were cast
as nefarious enemies of good, Christian Italians. As their
Jewish neighbors were persecuted, it was the rare non-
Jewish Italian who spoke up for them. More commonly,
former friends crossed the street to avoid having to greet
them. Italian academics showed themselves all too eager
to benefit from the openings created when their Jewish colleagues were cast out and, indeed, following the
war, fought mightily to resist giving their positions back
to them.

Italy's antisemitic campaign, beginning two years before Italy entered the war, can properly be placed alongside the antisemitic campaign in these years in Germany
(and elsewhere in central Europe) as a crucial step in the
process that would make the Holocaust possible. Before
people could entertain the idea of sending Jewish children and other defenseless Jews to their death, simply
for being Jewish, they first had to rob them of their humanity, to cast them as dangerous enemies. This the Italians did with the imposition of the racial laws.

The antisemitic campaign facilitated the mass murder
of Italy's Jews in another way as well, as Levis Sullam

shows, for it created both a census of all of the Jews and a bureaucracy devoted to their surveillance and persecution. As he notes in these pages, the roundup of France's Jews was slowed by the lack of documentation on who the Jews were and where they lived. The Italians had no such problem, thanks to the racial laws and the antisemitic government machinery that had been in place for five years before the roundups began.

An important part of Italians' ability to distance themselves from this past has been the creation of the myth of the "good Italian." Levis Sullam shows that this myth was constructed very early, beginning in the final months of the war, as Italians quickly remade their identities to cast themselves on the side of the war's victors. In this convenient narrative, Italians had only positive feelings for their Jewish fellow citizens. All of the horrible things done to the Jews were the work of the evil Germans, notwithstanding the Italians' own heroic efforts to protect them.

Insofar as the Holocaust is concerned, this myth relies both on the erasure of the five years of the Italian state campaign against the Jews in the years leading up to the Shoah and on the misrepresentation of how it was that those thousands of Jews in Italy in 1943–45 came to be identified, located, and transported to the death camps.

The Roman Catholic Church has been among the institutions with the greatest stake in this historical misrepresentation. In the Holy See's official version of this history, contained in the 1998 Vatican statement "We Remember," the antisemitism that led to the Holocaust was wholly distinct from the "religious" anti-Judaism that the Church had promulgated. As Levis Sullam shows, while this is a comforting account, it bears no relation to the actual history of the demonization of the Jews that was employed to justify their mass murder. The case Levis Sullam offers of a prominent Venetian physician who whipped up public sentiment against the Jewish threat is emblematic. His published screeds blended pseudoscience with classic Christian warnings of the terrible "divine punishment" that awaited the Jews, who had continued to remain "distant from Christ." Likewise, the most important Fascist state vehicle for spreading hatred of Italy's Jews, the twice-a-month illustrated publication *La difesa della razza*, was filled with traditional Christian tropes demonizing the Jews, from well poisoning to ritual murder.

Levis Sullam is able to draw on a number of important recent studies, along with published first-person testimonies, to show the crucial role Italians played in the roundup of Jews beginning in the fall of 1943. Of all the Jews sent to their death from Italy, half were seized not by German soldiers but by Italians. Moreover, in those cases where it was German soldiers who took them, the Germans relied on Italians to help them locate the Jews in their midst. In such cases, Italians often accompanied the Germans for this purpose.

In all this, Italy's own state machinery played a key role. Levis Sullam documents how both the Italian prefectures and the police departments were centrally involved in the roundup of Jews. Many Jews were then sent to Italy's own concentration camp, at Fossoli, run exclusively by Italian authorities, before being sent on trains run by the Italian rail service on their way to their death at Auschwitz.

As Levis Sullam laments, the industry of historical representation devoted to these events in Italy—the commercial films, the documentaries, the school lessons, the regular annual days of commemoration—draws attention not to the many thousands of Italians directly involved in the murder of Italy's Jews but to the courageous few who took risks to try to save them. Nor has this been simply a matter of state practice, for professional historians have also been influential in this casting of history.

Here, as Levis Sullam notes, the most influential of all Italian historians of Fascism, Renzo De Felice, has played a significant role. Before he set out on his massive, multivolume biography of Mussolini, De Felice published his *Storia degli ebrei italiani sotto il fascismo* (1961). In that seminal work, republished many times, he argued that Italians rejected antisemitism, claiming that it was not part of their culture. He likewise offered support for juxtaposing the good Italians with the evil Germans.

One of the key strands of Levis Sullam's account in these pages—and one that many readers will find perplexing—relates to the fact that De Felice and others who have made this argument have been able to justify it partly on testimony offered by Italian Jews. In the immediate postwar period, following the years the Jewish survivors had spent being treated as enemies of their Christian neighbors, and the trauma they had suffered, there was a great desire to be brought back into the national community. Treating the persecution they had endured not as the work of true Italians but of some kind of foreign agent offered the Jews a path that was convenient for all concerned. The fact that during the *ventennio* many

Jewish Italians had embraced Fascism, along with their Christian neighbors, added an interest in the rewriting of history that made this narrative all the more appealing.

Following the war, the great majority of Italians found guilty of war crimes were pardoned, and almost all of the relative few who were not served short sentences before being released. As Levis Sullam details in these pages, far from being punished, some went on to receive the state's highest honors. Telling is the case of the jurist Gaetano Azzariti, who served as the president of the special tribunal overseeing the racial laws from 1938 to 1943, responsible for the persecution of Italy's Jews. No sooner had Mussolini been toppled in July 1943 than Azzariti was appointed by Italy's new prime minister to be minister of justice. The following decade, Azzariti was named to Italy's Constitutional Court, becoming its president in 1957, a position he held at the top of Italy's judiciary until his death four years later. Until recently, his bust adorned the hall of that court.

As Levis Sullam notes, no Italians were sentenced after the war for their participation in the persecution of the Jews and only a handful at most for their role in the roundup of the Jews for deportation to the death camps. The fact that the people judging their cases were, for the most part, the same men who served in the judiciary that oversaw the Fascist State and its racial laws offers some insight into the nature of Italy's postwar efforts to come to terms with its crimes and responsibilities.

Indeed, Italy has yet to come to terms with its uncomfortable past. As Levis Sullam points out, there has been no assumption of responsibility by the Italian state or its police force for the persecution of Italy's Jews, or for their murder. Although the state dutifully observes a day of memory, what is remembered is not the participation of thousands of Italians in the mass murder of Italy's Jews but a very different, more comforting history. Perhaps it is too much to ask that for future annual commemoration of the Holocaust Italians be asked to read Simon Levis Sullam's book.

DAVID I. KERTZER

July 14, 2017

The Italian Executioners

Prologue

An Evening in 1943

On the evening of Saturday, December 5, 1943, a few hours before the roundup of Jews in Venice that would lead to the arrest of over 160 men, women, and children, the young pianist Arturo Benedetti Michelangeli gave a concert at the Teatro La Fenice. The following day, a few hours after the arrested Jews had been temporarily detained in the local prisons, the city's soccer team played a match at the Sant'Elena stadium. The arrests had occurred during the night, in a city under a government-imposed blackout, in the middle of a particularly harsh winter.[1] As the genocide of the Jews was beginning in Venice, the days passed as usual, with life and death mingling indistinguishably. Perhaps the prefect who had issued the order to arrest the Jews had afterward attended the concert given by Michelangeli. And one of the police officers or Fascist volunteers who made those arrests may have attended the game at the stadium just a few hours later.

Even in the context of total war and civil war, the majority of events, both of those two days and of the following months, were well integrated into the ordinariness of daily life. Yet other events seemed to respond to a different logic, completely new and, as it were, reversed: that of genocide. This rationale led the police, the upholders of order and safety, to arrest a segment of the population, now considered foreign and hostile, on the basis of their origins and affiliation. It also led, a few weeks later, to the transfer of a group of Jewish minors from Venice to the concentration and transit camp of Fossoli di Carpi, both to be reunited with their parents who had been briefly detained there and to ensure that they would share the fate of their families, who soon after were deported by the Germans to Auschwitz for extermination.

In German-occupied Venice, the cultural capital of Salò and the hub of the embassies to the newborn Repubblica Sociale Italiana (Italian Social Republic [RSI]), safe from the bombings and therefore overcrowded, movie theaters were open, hotels were packed, and people danced at parties and clubs.[2] In the center of the city, amid the hustle and bustle, a Jewish collaborator and the police officer working with him to make some extra cash attempted to spot any Jews who had escaped identification and arrest in order to turn them in to the Italian police or, for the right price, directly to the Germans. Schools were open, books and newspapers were printed, and lectures were given. One lecture was held in the Ala Napoleonica, a neoclassical building overlooking St. Mark's Square. Thronged by a well-educated and engaged audience, it was given by an eminent Venetian doctor. The topic was the "Jews," the "disease of humanity."[3] High culture and even science had combined with propaganda to justify and support the ongoing genocide. There was no need for the speaker to explicitly describe what was happening to the Jews. He had only to evoke the "danger" lurking everywhere, the "betrayal" to be avenged, and the "evil" to be eradicated. It was enough to allude to the just, inevitable fate awaiting anyone who implemented or personified this evil. For more than five years, since the introduction of antisemitic laws in 1938, Fascism through its political means, administrations, and propaganda had succeeded in transforming the "defense of the race" into a crucial issue, formulaic and diffuse throughout totalitarian Italian society—the raging war only serving to press the issue further. At the same time, antisemitism had become a matter of ordinary governance—even to the people who only read about it in the newspapers. It was a matter entrusted to the state bureaucracy, to the police agencies, and to the Fascist Party's military bodies, and it persisted in Salò at an even higher level of radical commitment, directly involving thousands of Italians at varying degrees of responsibility and awareness.

This book maintains that, from 1943 to 1945, the Italians who declared the Jews "foreigners" and "enemies," segregating and persecuting them on the basis of their race, hunting them house by house, arresting them, imprisoning them, ransacking their goods and belongings, transporting them and holding them in concentration camps and transit camps, and finally handing them over to the Germans, were, in fact, responsible for genocide.

Genocide is defined as a violent effort to eradicate a group, in whole or in part, on the basis of ethnicity or race. Although the final acts of extermination were not carried out on Italian soil or by Italian hands, there is no doubt that Italians, working both at the center and on the periphery of the reborn Fascist State, also took the initiative in the process. While their involvement varied in degree and method, according to their different roles, practical contributions, and modes of participation, each act furthered the planning and execution of the annihilation of the Jews. Through each decision, understanding, and action Italians became agents of and accomplices to the Holocaust.

The term "genocide" was coined during the course of the extermination of the Jews by Raphael Lemkin, a Polish Jewish jurist and émigré to the United States, to define what was happening in eastern Europe (Lemkin had also applied the term to prior events such as the genocide of the Armenians).[4] The term was first introduced into international law in 1948 at the Convention for the Prevention and Punishment of the Crime of Genocide. Its usage in reference to the Shoah and similar events of comparable destructive intent, both prior and subsequent, has gradually increased, including by historians, especially since the 1990s.[5] The word "genocide" in reference to the extermination of the Jews is, in some respects, more neutral than both "Holocaust," which evokes an etymological notion of the sacrificial, and "Shoah," which seems to exclude the affected non-Jewish groups. At the same time, the term "genocide" allows for a comparison of similar causes and effects, and emphasizes, by analogy with the legal definition of crime, the intent, which in this case is the endeavor to partially or completely destroy a national, ethnic, racial, or religious group.

These, therefore, are the terms with which the genocide of the Jews and Italian accountability should be discussed. Culpability does not belong only to those who personally carried out the arrests: police, *carabinieri* (Italian military police), customs officers, members of the militia or of the National Republican Guard (GNR), and

Fascist volunteers. It also belongs to those who compiled the lists of victims: from the municipal and state employees at the racial registry office to the police officials who took the names from the lists and placed them on arrest warrants; from the prefect and chief of police who signed the warrants, all the way down the hierarchical ladder to the typists who prepared the documents. Participants and accomplices too were those who seized and confiscated Jewish property, spending hours, sometimes even days, describing in the minutest details the impounded goods, storing them under lock and key, shipping them to other offices or departments, or—not infrequently—keeping them for personal use or to sell for a quick profit. Additionally there were the informers: those who identified, reported, delivered, and betrayed Jewish victims, their own fellow citizens, sometimes even their own friends and neighbors. Thus unfolds the chain of responsibility through multiple, if sometimes seemingly innocuous, stages and actions: from those who conducted the trucks, buses, or boats that transferred the prisoners; to those who monitored the cells or the transit camps; to those who built the camps or supplied them with provisions. Lastly, there were those who stood by and did nothing, turning their attention away, choosing to ignore what was happening, preoccupied with and sometimes overwhelmed by other things, by daily hardships and by the tragedies of the ongoing war. The degrees of participation in the genocide by these individuals, including those who performed the arrests and those who transcribed the lists of Jews to be arrested, were not the same and, undoubtedly, the use of legal and judicial terms in historical context could assist in designating their various levels of involvement and guilt based on each individual's specific function, role in the hierarchy, and awareness or lack thereof of genocidal intentions and of their ultimate results.[6] However, the objectives of a historian are not those of a judge. By using the term "genocide" with an emphasis on the responsibility of the Italians we intend to focus our attention on the plan, on the series of actions, and on the methods of participation that we clearly see repeated time after time but also on the gravity of acts that, though typically evaluated individually, were actually part of the larger process of extermination and that have been underscrutinized for too long. If the responsibilities of the Italian executioners appear clearly different from those of the people who personally murdered their victims, it may be useful to remember the observations of Raul Hilberg: "It must be kept in mind that most of the participants [of the Shoah] did not fire rifles at Jewish children or pour gas into gas chambers. A good many, of course, also had to perform these very 'hard' tasks, but most of the administrators and most of the clerks did not see the final, drastic link in these measures of destruction. Most bureaucrats composed memoranda, drew up blueprints, signed correspondence, talked on the telephone, and participated in conferences. They could destroy a whole people by sitting at their desks." These remarks, which are applicable beyond their bureaucratic connotations, were quoted by Zygmunt Bauman, who stressed that "causal connections between their actions and the mass murder were difficult to spot,"[7] and this made their work easier. It reduced the personal responsibility of the actors, so that they could each perform the tasks and play the parts necessary to carry out the genocide of the Jews.

Between the fall of 1943 and the spring of 1945, amid the ravages of the raging world war and civil war, thousands of Italians participated in the destruction of the Jews, delivering more than six thousand victims to their deaths. This began after five years of persecution that had started in 1938 and had isolated and segregated the Jewish group, labeled them inferior, and, finally, sought to eliminate them from the country altogether.[8] As we will see, efforts to diminish or expunge Italian participation in the deportation of the Jews began in the immediate aftermath of the war, in particular, on the part of the Italian Ministry of Foreign Affairs and its diplomatic body. As early as 1946, an amnesty prevented thousands of trials for Fascist crimes from taking place. This created a paucity of investigations and led to a "fact-finding vacuum"[9] and thus a dearth of information about Italian actions during the Holocaust. In the few trials that did actually occur, anti-Jewish persecution did not constitute a specific offense and was therefore not usually taken into consideration. (This was also the case in the postwar trials at Nuremberg.) The early international historiography of the Holocaust systematically offered a benevolent representation of the role of Italians in the "Final Solution" and even claimed that the Italian national character was unsuited to commit any crime. Moreover, Italian Jewish institutions, seeking to acknowledge the help received by many Jews during the war, placed the greatest emphasis on Italian rescue efforts. These factors, as we will see in the concluding chapter, all served to undermine the seriousness of the actions of the Italian persecutors and permitted their stories to recede into the shadows.

In the following pages, I will examine the backgrounds and motivations of the Italians who contributed to the genocide of the Jews.[10] Their roles, especially in recent years, have been downplayed and replaced by those of the Italians who acted as saviors, thus risking that history will remember only the victims and heroes while increasingly, or even completely, overlooking the persecutors. This book will reclaim those stories from the shadows and bring to light the actions of the Italian executioners.

One

THE IDEOLOGICAL CONTEXT OF GENOCIDE

By the time civil war broke out in Italy in the fall of 1943,[1] Fascism had been vilifying the Jews for five years. Starting with the 1938 enactment of antisemitic laws, it had gradually excluded Jews from numerous areas of Italian society, teaching Italians to consider the Jewish race inferior. Although antisemitism had occasionally been invoked by Mussolini and Fascism in the first half of the 1920s, it was only as Italian society became more totalitarian from the mid-1930s onward that anti-Jewish tendencies appeared more systematically.[2] Antisemitism emerged in the extremist fringes of the movement—in the pages of Roberto Farinacci's newspaper *Il Regime fascista*, for example—as well as in the form of episodes involving national cultural institutions or local administrations within the regime.[3] The conquest of Ethiopia in 1936 had added fuel to the fire of the collective racist imagination, which, starting in 1937, manifested itself through measures of "racial prophylaxis" intended to prevent unions between Italian colonizers and colonized Africans.[4] In that year, the Fascist regime had started down the path of state racism and antisemitism,

and the summer of 1938 saw the publication of a manifesto by the so-called "racial scientists" that proclaimed
the superiority of the Italian race. It was followed that
autumn by the enactment of laws expelling Jews from
schools and public administration and severely limit-
ing the professional practices, business activities, and
property ownership of Jews. These provisions included
a racist "purge" of the publishing industry and libraries,
which prohibited the publication and even the loan of
works by Jewish authors.[5] It also included measures conceived by a relentless and absurd bureaucracy intended
to socially humiliate the Jews, such as excluding them
from certain beaches.[6] Yet another measure prevented
Jews from participating in associations for the protection
of animals.[7] In this way, the Italian society forming under
the new totalitarian system of Fascism, pervaded by the
Fascist ideal of a "new man," was a society founded—to
borrow an expression from a different context—on racial
"apartheid" in the colonies and on antisemitism at home.
This regime was not conceived as a temporary digres-
sion but rather as the new and enduring face of modern
Italy, designed to last. This antisemitic and racist change
in direction began to transform the way Italian society
portrayed itself, shaping a culture based on racial separation and bombarding public opinion via the media,
propaganda, and high culture, thus producing genera-
tions of Italians who were force-fed racist ideas by their
schools and by the propaganda machine.[8] These ideas
settled atop an existing stratum of age-old religious prejudices inspired by Catholic anti-Judaism that was present in the most diverse areas of Italian society, even in the
most secular spheres.[9] With the exception of the brief

interruption of General Pietro Badoglio's forty-five days in power following the toppling of Mussolini in July 1943 (during which the racist measures were still not lifted), the officially sanctioned antisemitism of 1938 provided a continuous legal, political, cultural, and ideological context in which the most radical measures of the anti-Jewish policy of the Social Republic of Salò would make their appearance. While the antisemitism of 1938 cannot be directly linked to the genocidal shift of 1943–45, it is safe to say that it provided the background necessary for such a shift to take hold.

The fall of Mussolini, the end of the regime, and the about-face in military alliances in the summer of 1943 (the Italians left the Germans and joined forces with the Allies) triggered accusations of betrayal and elevated the figure of the traitor in the popular imagination. A fixation with traitors would take on a key role in the revived Fascism of September 1943.[10] Moreover, the concept of betrayal and traitors overlapped with the conspiracy theories typical of the antisemitic tradition. The flames of war, especially fratricidal war, were fanned by fears of the enemy within, and the figure of the Jew, now identified by the genocidal shift as enemy and target, had already been singled out for centuries in Europe as the "stranger within." Mussolini's renewed alliance with Nazism at the very time in which it was promoting its project of mass destruction caused the Fascism of Salò, in its ideological radicalization, to once again focus on the antisemitism it had embraced in 1938 as a renewed political resource and as one of the self-defining fundamentals of the new Fascist Social Republic. Article 7 of the Manifesto of Verona, which set out the principles and aims of the

Republic of Salò, therefore defined the Jews as foreigners and enemies, paving the way for their persecution, for their imprisonment, and for their deportation.

Scholars of civil wars have remarked that "every conflict of this type triggers a mechanism causing those who were supposedly 'one of us' to become strangers whom it is legitimate, necessary, and urgent to harm even to the point of annihilation." "The dehumanization of the adversary," moreover, "becomes necessary to preserving the sense of self."[11] On the other hand, in civil war "there are greater feelings of equality or shared past, languages and places, and more frequent transitions, camouflaging, duplicity, and changing of sides than among soldiers in a foreign army. But, indeed, the most foreign of all is the foreigner within."[12] At the same time civil war sociology has drawn attention to the link between civil war and intimacy. Unlike interstate conflicts, this type of war is characterized by proximity, commonality, and affinity. As we shall see, informing plays a crucial role in this context as a "micro-foundation of intimate violence."[13] This also forces us to reflect on the relationship between intimacy and genocide that developed in the context of the civil war from 1943 to 1945. Genocide does not necessarily occur—on the contrary occurs less frequently—in distant, foreign lands than in our own society, among the kindred, among the familiar, even among next-door neighbors. In fact, those closest to us are usually the first to become informers or even executioners.[14]

The observations made by anthropologist Mary Douglas apply even more profoundly. She notes that apprehension regarding purity and danger in unstable situations enables the construction or reconstruction of a symbolic order. In Salò, too, segregation and elimination were used to deal with the anxiety created by extreme conditions and instability, and to create or reestablish the appearance of order. "Ideas about separating, purifying, demarcating and punishing transgressions have as their main function to impose system on an inherently untidy experience," notes Douglas. "It is only by exaggerating the difference between within and without, about and below, male and female, with and against, that a semblance of order is created." And the "initial recognition of anomaly leads to anxiety and from there to suppression or avoidance."[15] If we were to paraphrase Douglas, we might say that under "disorderly" and "dangerous" conditions society needs to be "purified" through the imposition of an "exaggerated" "order" based on "separation," on being either "with" or "against." In the racist vision, the presumed otherness represents the contaminating anomaly that causes anxiety and, by way of reaction, avoidance or—in the genocidal situation—elimination. The ideal of the RSI was structured on notions of "us" versus "them" and distinguished the "pure" from the "impure," thus leading to their annihilation. It laid the ideological and propagandistic groundwork necessary to prepare, justify, and support the conflict of civil war and participation in the Shoah.

The anti-Jewish theories and propaganda of the reincarnated Fascist State will here be illustrated through three figures representing different levels of action and responsibility during 1943–45: Giovanni Preziosi, an ideologist and theorist during Italy's twenty-year Fascist period, then a man of the government, an aspiring legislator, and propagandist in the RSI; the bureaucrat and executioner Giovanni Martelloni, "expert" writer on the "Jewish question" and head of the Office of Jewish Affairs in Florence; and the distinguished radiologist Giocondo Protti, who became an antisemitic lecturer and hack.

Let us begin by opening the pages of the publications of Salò—daily newspapers, magazines, and books—and reviving the voices therein. "By the way, where can one buy *Bolscevismo, Plutocrazia e Massoneria* [Bolshevism, plutocracy and freemasonry] by Giovanni Preziosi, published and distributed by Mondadori? And where can one find the *Protocols of the Elders of Zion* sold exclusively in Italy by Baldini and Castoldi?" These words concluded a short article dated March 18, 1944, titled "Il ritorno di Preziosi" (The return of Preziosi), which appeared in the first issue of *Avanguardia Europea*, the weekly magazine published by Italian SS volunteers. The article referred to a long, cordial meeting that Preziosi had recently had with Mussolini and announced the creation of the General Inspectorate of Race, personally directed by Preziosi with the aim of carrying out a "drastic and systematic purge of the national character," inspired by the theory that "the tragic situation in which the Fatherland found itself was exclusively due to masonic and Judaic plots."[16] The Social Republic was therefore responsible for reinstating Preziosi, defrocked priest, journalist, and agitator. Even before Fascism's rise to power, he had produced the first Italian translation of the *Protocols of the Elders of Zion* (1921), republished in 1937 and 1938, and again in 1944–45, in three editions, one by the Ministry of Culture. Preziosi had also edited the magazine *La Vita Italiana*—another product revived by the RSI[17]—which had, throughout the twenty years of Fascism, peddled the themes of the international Jewish conspiracy and the traditionalist esoteric racism advanced by its main theorist, Julius Evola, to which Preziosi added a specific "biological-mystic" component.[18] After the fall of Fascism in July 1943, the former priest and racist propagandist had fled to Germany, where he was received by Hitler himself in his headquarters and where, in September 1943, with German support, he began broadcasting his own radio propaganda show live from Munich to Italy. Preziosi renewed his contacts with Mussolini in early December 1943, sending him a number of articles that he had published in the *Völkischer Beobachter* (the Nazi newspaper edited by Alfred Rosenberg), explaining to the Germans how Freemasons and Jews had caused the fall of Fascism and supporting a "profound purge of the Freemasons" as well as a "comprehensive solution to the Jewish question." At the end of January 1944, Preziosi submitted a memorandum to Il Duce in which he reiterated his unwavering dedication to the steady denunciation of the pernicious role of Freemasonry and Judaism, reminding Mussolini, who was at that time engaged in setting up the Republic of Salò, of a prophetically sinister phrase in Hitler's *Mein Kampf*: "Our first task is not to create a national State constitution, but to eliminate the Jews. [. . .] The main difficulty lies, not in forming the new state of things, but in making space for them."[19]

In March 1944, the General Inspectorate of Race began its activities, directed by Preziosi with the support of a twenty-one-person staff. The Inspectorate was responsible for identifying "racial status," providing information on Freemasonry, the "plutocracy," and hidden political forces; promoting and studying "racial questions," especially the Jewish question; supervising the confiscation of Jewish property; and diffusing antisemitic propaganda in Italian schools and in the review titled *Razza e civiltà*, which had returned to publication and had become the Inspectorate's mouthpiece.[20] At the same time Preziosi also developed a series of proposals intended to harshen antisemitic legislation by extending persecutory provisions to "mixed bloods" and "half-breeds," whether foreign or Italian, and creating new "genealogical files" for the individual certification of one's "Italian blood." Many aspects of the organization of the Inspectorate and of the political and legislative proposals developed by Preziosi evoked the Nazi model, often making explicit reference to it. Moreover, at the time of his proposal to introduce a "comprehensive solution to the Jewish problem," Preziosi was undoubtedly aware of the solution adopted by the Germans, and, at the very latest by the fall of 1943, during his stay in Germany, he would have had occasion to learn its details firsthand. In his memorandum to Mussolini, he also wrote:

> The first task to be tackled is not the so-called "national concord" that [philosopher Giovanni] Gentile and others keep blathering on about, but the total elimination of the Jews, starting with those, and they are no small number, revealed in the census of August 1938, which has never been made public. Then we need to track down those who are more or less baptized or aryanized. Then we need to exclude mixed-bloods, husbands of Jewesses, and anyone with a drop of Jewish blood in their

veins from the ganglion of national life, from the army, from the magistracy, from the teaching profession, and from both the central and peripheral hierarchies of the Party. The same applies to anyone belonging to the Freemasons.[21]

Considered together, these new legislative proposals and renewed political imperatives amounted to nothing less than a warrant for genocide, conceived—and by that time already launched—as a joint Italian-German undertaking.

In June 1944, following the Allied advance from the south, Giovanni Martelloni moved north from Florence where he had directed the prefecture's Office of Jewish Affairs to join the Inspectorate of Race. From the time of the rebirth of Fascism in the Republic of Salò, Martelloni, whose career will be described in detail in another chapter, had performed a dual role both resuming and expanding the work that he had carried out since 1941 as an antisemitic writer and journalist with scholarly aspirations and working as a persecutor of Jews. He personally carried out arrests and confiscations in Florence where the prefect had put him in charge of coordinating the anti-Jewish activities conducted by Fascists in the city and province.

Martelloni was also the author of a series of articles published in the daily newspaper *Il Nuovo Giornale* between January and May 1944. They were based on a hypothesized historical reconstruction of the Jewish presence in Florence, describing the Jews' arrival in the city in the fifteenth century and the beginnings of their moneylending activities. The articles mingled a pseudoscientific reconstruction based on studies and documents with prejudices and stereotypes drawing upon anti-Judaic theology as well as antisemitism.[22] In an article published in February 1944 Martelloni explored the conversion of the Jews, defined as a "current topic," intending to demonstrate the validity of the most recent legislation that punished Jews "even if baptized, or exonerated,"[23] given that "even if they are converted, they continue to be Jewish, to reveal themselves as Jewish, and to boast of being Jewish." He ended the article by affirming that "such considerations should not be a cue for violent individual attacks upon these Jews, but for the occasion to envisage, definitively and positively—once and for all—a solution to the problem that has plagued the world for two thousand years: 'the Jewish problem.' A complex problem that no purification ritual can or could hope to resolve or alleviate. A problem that can be defined as a real and true 'danger': a cultural, spiritual, and tangible danger as proven by the war underway."[24] In April 1944, Martelloni published the booklet *La confisca dei beni ebraici* (The confiscation of Jewish assets), in which he accompanied the Legislative Decree of January 4, 1944, with a historical premise and a comment on the role of the antisemitic official and expert. The booklet illustrated "the historic continuity of the defensive feeling against the danger of Jewish corruption of our national mentality, by Rome and by the Church in the modern age." It concluded by affirming the historical necessity of the recent legislation—and therefore of the persecution—because of the responsibility of the Jews for "having unleashed upon the world that terrible storm of hatred, iron, and blood that is currently raging around us."[25]

Lastly, prominent among the antisemitic propagandists active from 1943 to 1945 was Giocondo Protti, a well-known doctor in Venice who had been an enthusiastic promoter of racist legislation since at least the early 1940s in his dual role as chairman of the provincial union of the Fascist Confederation of Professionals and Artists and provincial secretary of the Fascist Union of Physicians.[26] After the establishment of the Social Republic, Protti assumed the role of lecturer and antisemitic writer, both in the city of Venice and for some of the varied and polycentric periodicals and publications generated by the Republic of Salò, receiving praise and possibly even funds from the Nazis. The nature of Protti's antisemitism, which combined Catholic anti-Judaism with a biological racism inspired by his training and scientific activity, was showcased in an article concerning the talk that he gave in Venice in the fall of 1943 titled "The Jews as the Disease of Humanity" and in *Il dramma di Israele* (The tragedy of Israel), an essay examining some aspects of his own talk in greater depth that appeared in *Orizzonti*, the single issue published by Edizioni Erre in 1944.[27] From the beginning, Protti alluded to the persecution underway at that time: "Someone remarked to me that it is exceedingly mean-spirited to criticize the Jews today, because it is uncharitable to rage against the oppressed." But his talk intended to demolish that point of view ("We, unfortunate 'gentiles' are the ones suffering under their centuries-old, secretive, and mocking yoke") and provided historical justifications for that persecution. This evidence was mainly taken from the "celebrated and terrifying *Protocols of the Elders of Zion*" and on their "fearsome evidentiary power." The *Protocols* revealed the immense strength of the "corrosion and infiltration" of the Jews and their aspirations to wealth and political control, the pursuit of which was overseen by "chief rabbis who were the brains of an international system." The failure to recognize Christ had caused a "congenital mutilation of the spirit" in the Jews that could not be reversed even after baptism—Protti claimed that, on this, the Church and the Germans found themselves in agreement. The Jews had caused the current war and represented an incurable illness for society: "The Jew, therefore, may be considered a spiritual monstrosity afflicting the soul of the world in the same way that cancer is a biological monstrosity which invades the healthy flesh of humankind," wrote the doctor. A "great, cathartic divine punishment" therefore awaited the Jews "who had remained far from Christ," concluded Protti: a punishment "that would once more be without remedy or possibility of escape."[28] In a report sent from Venice in the spring of 1944, the German consul mentioned that this piece on the "tragedy of Israel" had grown out of a lecture that had been met with public acclaim when it was held at the Ateneo Veneto—the local academy and lecture hall—under the auspices of the Fascist Institute of Culture. The consul also identified Protti as one of the first supporters of the RSI in Venice and as a contributor to *Il Regime fascista*, the newspaper published by the Fascist extremist Roberto Farinacci. The Nazi diplomat expressed his hopes that such initiatives might be repeated and clearly considered the Venetian doctor a reliable collaborator.[29]

Surveys carried out in the Salò press confirm that antisemitism was one of the defining aspects of RSI propaganda and ideology, and a locus of self-identity in the civil war that justified the anti-Jewish persecution, providing it with motivational support. The inherent self-defining function of antisemitism is confirmed by the fact that even when most of the Jewish arrests had already taken place, antisemitic propaganda continued to proclaim a crazed "antisemitism without Jews."[30] As we shall see, the demand for new, radical, anti-Jewish measures coincided with the rebirth of Fascism from September 1943 onward. That autumn, the Fascist press exacerbated matters, calling for violence against the enemy within: "By now, extreme measures are the only thing worth using against the invading enemy, against his accomplices on the inside: the Jews and the anti-fascists," claimed *Il Fascio*, the weekly newspaper published by the Republican Fascist Party in Milan, on November 12, 1943. Two days earlier the Como newspaper *La provincia* had written the following about the Jews: "They were the main instigators of this war and it would be criminal not to act accordingly, applying maximum pressure and not falling victim to foolish sentimentalism."[31] Shortly after the start of the deportations, *Rivoluzione*, Padua's Republican Fascist newspaper, thundered: "For many years the Jews have been poisoning the life of the world as part of a deranged plan for world domination." The Blackshirts of the Ettore Muti action squad led the charge to "morally and physically kill all the Jews"—let us "make a clean sweep. Away with them! Death to them all! Confiscate all of their property." They reminded the "soft-hearted" and the "do-gooders" or anyone believing that many Jews had been "good comrades" during the twenty years of Fascism or who was convinced that some of the "heads" of Padua's Fascist movement "were almost Jewish or Jewish sympathizers," that these same Jews had helped topple the regime, funded anti-Fascism, and "hatched plots in every sphere to hinder our rebuilding of the Fatherland."[32] Ideas regarding the "Jewish conspiracy" and the Jews as an "enemy race," widely present in the extreme Fascist press in Tuscany,[33] were rekindled when the conflict broke out in order to blame the Jews for the war.[34] The presence of African American soldiers among the U.S. troops following the Allied landings inspired Salò Fascism to dust off its anti-African racism, representing the invaders as beastly and sexually voracious both in its press and in its visual propaganda.[35] The militant press expressed its approval of the use of persecutory measures including deportation and seizure of Jewish property in articles such as the one published in Farinacci's *Il Regime fascista* (the newspaper involved in anti-Jewish campaigns since at least 1935) under the succinct heading: "Radical Solution."[36] Likely acting under orders for official Fascist propaganda, the local daily press had joined the choir of voices favoring persecutory measures: thus daily newspapers like the *Gazzetta dell'Emilia* of Bologna and *L'Arena* of Verona praised the order for the arrest of the Jews for its "revolutionary swiftness" ("further proof of the Republican government's decision to destroy at the root those evils that have caused Italy so much, too much harm").[37] Venice's daily *Il Gazzettino* described the Jews as "enemies who, whether concealed or overt, have now been unmasked by the powers of the new Europe," defining the orders against them to be "necessary" and "decisive" and ending with the following claim: "In our country too, the Jewish conspiracy has taken things too far: so far in fact that those responsible have received the punishment that they deserve."[38] Also participating in the anti-Jewish journalistic campaign of that time were national papers, rededicated to Fascism, such as *La Stampa*, which called for Jews to "pay the penalty for being anti-Italian"[39] while the *Corriere della Sera*'s smug comment associated Judaism with conspiracies: "As the roundups and segregation of our diehard enemies proceed, we can expect a substantial decrease in spying and terrorist acts. The strings pulling the various conspiracies will snap as if by magic."[40]

The anti-Jewish polemic was as present in the Fascist press, the mouthpiece of militants, functionaries, and the higher echelons of the Social Republic, as in the papers combining Catholicism with Fascism (*Crociata Italica* and *Italia Cattolica*) and in cultural reviews like *Italia e Civiltà* edited in Florence by Barna Occhini, the son-in-law of the Catholic writer Giovanni Papini. But antisemitism also pervaded the political imagination of the senior leaders and ministers of the Fascist Republic: not just the zealous Giovanni Preziosi but even former members of Mussolini's circle like Nicola Bombacci, who returned to the scene publishing a pamphlet in Padua in August 1944 that denounced the Jewish roots of Bolshevism he had become acquainted with in Russia during his pro-Communist phase. Similarly, we find anti-Judaism seeping from the pages drafted by Minister of Popular Culture Fernando Mezzasoma, who accused the Italian government born in southern Italy in September 1943, and its vice-chairman, "the monarchist Communist" To-gliatti, of serving the "Judeo-Masonic plutocracy." Book titles such as *Ecco gli ebrei* (Here are the Jews), *La finanza ebraica alla conquista dei paesi arabi* (The role of Jewish finance in conquering Arab countries), and *La questione giudaica vista dai Cattolici oltre cinquant'anni fa* (The Jewish question as seen by Catholics over fifty years ago) pepper the catalogues of the publishing house Edizioni Popolari, which printed them in Venice and in the Veneto region between 1944 and 1945.[41] These publications were hand-books or summaries that revived various veins of the anti-Jewish tradition. *Ecco gli ebrei*, for example, begins with an introduction that bundles conspiracy theories in the style of the *Protocols of the Elders of Zion*, religious anti-Judaism, and criticisms of Jewish sympathizers, followed by an anthology containing pages of anti-Jewish con-tent taken from celebrated works and authors. Excerpts taken from the *Protocols* themselves, from the Jesuit *Civiltà Cattolica*, and from the Vatican's *Osservatore Romano* are ac-companied by a random series of citations from authors such as Fichte, Kant, Preziosi, Jabalot, Guerrazzi, Herder, Leopardi, Oriani, Drumont, Cogni, Lemann, Henry Ford, and Lamennais.[42]

In addition to this propaganda, from 1938 onward the existence of a racist, antisemitic pedagogy is well doc-umented in Italian education, especially of the youth. What is harder to evaluate is the effectiveness of the dif-fusion and the reception of antisemitism. It was clearly part of the officers' training in the Fascist National Repub-lican Guard (Guardia Nazionale Repubblicana [GNR]) during the RSI. The acceptance of anti-Jewish theories and stereotypes by young recruits in the GNR has been documented by the discovery of materials in the archives produced for a "Racial-Political Culture Course" held from March to August 1944 in the Officer Cadet School at Fontanellato near Parma. The course was taught by Major Sergio D'Alba, son of GNR general Auro D'Alba, who was considered part of an extremist fringe of the RSI close to Giovanni Preziosi. The course was organized in three parts, each comprising a series of lectures with titles such as "Human Races," "Judaism and Freemasonry" (with subthemes such as the "semantic and spiritual character of the Jew," "systems of conflict in Judaism," and "the systematic disintegration of spiritual values in Aryan civilizations"), and "The Modern World and Its Wars" (based on historic themes of the day such as "the weapons and stages of the Judaic-Freemason attack on the European tradition," "Fascism as an attempt to return to an Aryan-Roman spirituality," and "the current war: clashes among worldviews and races"). The class required the students to hand in a final essay titled "How to Conceive a Racist Act in the RSI."

The course curriculum and the essays produced by the students document the syncretic intertwinement of antisemitic strands with spiritual and biological racism, elements of Catholic anti-Judaism, and references to Nazism as a model. They also contain confused and sketchily described anti-Jewish images borrowed from literature such as Giovanni Papini's novel *Gog* (published in 1931), along with Julius Evola's brand of esoteric racism in *Il mito del sangue* (The myth of blood), published in 1937.

The essays written by these students, aged nineteen to twenty-five, some of whom would soon meet their deaths in the final clashes of the civil war, show not only that they had absorbed various aspects of their politico-racist cultural lessons but that several years of propaganda along with a school curriculum that had inculcated them with the state's racism had left their mark as well. Many of them mixed racist concepts with the Fascist myth of ancient Rome, developing new racist combinations sometimes modeled on and sometimes critical of German racism. Some suggested adopting prophylactic "medical" or "sterilizing" measures to guarantee racial purity as well as pedagogical projects intended to reinforce "racial consciousness." Lastly, many affirmed the need for "total expulsion" or "the complete expulsion of Jews from every corner of national life."

G. M., a nineteen-year-old officer cadet, wrote, "In this case I would use decisive methods, without compromises or middle ground. Secrecy, surprise, stringency, complete eradication."[43] Such scenarios seem to have been inspired by the recent and ongoing anti-Jewish operations of the RSI and possibly by at least a partial awareness of the Nazi extermination underway at the time.

The same student also included stereotypical descriptions of the physical appearance and features of the Jew in his final exam: "frizzy hair, bovine eyes drowsily placid between eyelids and fat, jutting lower lip, classic unmistakable humped nose with large flared nostrils." He even envisions "a museum of artifacts" that would exhibit a "monstrous, grotesque, giant black fetus" in a cylindrical jar bearing the label "Aebreus maleficus" (Evil Jew).[44]

Such descriptions reveal the diffusion and success of anti-Jewish images and visual stereotypes, as well as of the propagation of anti-African ideas since the Fascist colonial enterprise in 1935–36, by now made even more monstrous and grotesque. Such images had already emerged in the racist campaigns of 1938–43, in periodicals such as the leading Fascist racist magazine *Difesa della razza* (Defense of the race), as well as in satirical reviews.[45] Starting at the outbreak of the conflict, and later continued by the RSI and Propagandastaffel, the Nazi propaganda service, it seems the diffusion of posters portraying Bolsheviks with Jewish features had spread: Jewish, Masonic, and Communist hands reach out to grab a terrorized Italian child in tears with the caption "Difendilo!" (Protect him!). In addition, depictions of threatening Jewish capitalists or wild, insatiable Africans decorated the walls of the Case del Fascio (Houses of the Fascio, the local headquarters of the Fascist party), the schools, the city streets, and the shop windows of the Republic of Salò. These public spaces were reclaimed by Fascism from 1943 to 1945.[46] One of the paradoxical and tragic functions of such images was to "visualize the invisible."[47] Exhibited during the course of the genocide itself, they not only depicted the plotting Jew and his plan for world domination but also showed the Jew who hid to escape persecution or, even worse, the Jew who had already been exterminated. At the beginning of the deportations, under the title *L'ebreo c'è ma non si vede* (The Jew is there but cannot be seen), the antisemitic ideologist Gino Sottochiesa, famous for his campaigns since the late 1930s, urged anyone with lingering doubts about that presence or who hesitated to take action: "We have to hunt them down without pity and without pause, because they represent the most serious threat of the present time, in which the Fatherland must wipe out all of its enemies."[48]

Although memoirs and testimonies from Salò have downplayed or outright denied the significance and extent of antisemitism in the Social Republic,[49] there can be no doubt about the prominence of anti-Jewish themes in the press, in publishing, in the messaging—including the visual and radio messaging—of the reborn Fascism. While the full scale of their diffusion has yet to be assessed based on the surviving documentation, the evidence so far demonstrates that it was considerable. The key political importance of labeling Jews "foreigners" and "enemies" was echoed in the constant repetition of prejudices, accusations, and antisemitic myths and the invocation of radical solutions as the mobilizing and defining factors behind the revived Fascist movement.

While this collective imagination prepared, guided, and justified Italian participation in the genocide, the majority of Italian executioners were not necessarily ideologically motivated. The genocide was widely carried out by bureaucratic means, through police measures and actions: actions that represented political imperatives for some, for others simply orders from superiors, and for yet others an opportunity for profit or vendetta. For some it meant the ordinary administration of official business, like drawing up a list, and for others it meant carrying out practical duties, like driving a truck or a train.

Two

The Dynamics of Genocide
Interpreting Actions, Motivations, and Contexts

"At the time of her capture, the terrified child, Emma Calò, aged 6, clung, weeping, to the clothes of the concierge, seeking help and protection. Moved by the sight, Mr. and Mrs. Berna begged the official to desist from his intentions, but he was adamant." A *carabinieri* report presented during the trial at the Extraordinary Courts of Assize described the scene that had taken place in an apartment block in Rome on March 15, 1944. Following a tip, the local commissioner of Public Security, accompanied by several agents in plainclothes, had gone to the address in order to arrest Enrica Calò, her four barely adolescent children, a nephew, and her elderly parents, who were all hiding on the ground floor of the building. While the police commissioner argued with the concierges, who initially denied all knowledge, then tried to persuade him to desist, little Emma attempted to hide. Wary of the concierges, the commissioner "personally searched for the child until he found her."[1] According to the concierge, she had attempted to save the little girl with the "tacit agreement of one of the agents. . . . But the relentless police commissioner searched for her exhaustively until he captured her." Enrica's nephew had also attempted to hide, but "the police commissioner stubbornly pursued the aforementioned sixteen-year-old boy until, through additional operations, he succeeded in capturing him prior to the [family's] deportation." Enrica Calò and one of her daughters were arrested and deported, dying in an unknown location; her other children and nephew died in Buchenwald, Ravensbrück, and Mauthausen; little Emma died in Auschwitz a couple of months after her arrest. Postwar, the commissioner was initially ousted but was later acquitted of all charges thanks to the activities that he claimed to have carried out on behalf of the Resistance. According to his own account, this one time he could not have acted differently because he had been placed under surveillance by the chief of police, Pietro Caruso, and would have jeopardized "the pursuit of his own sabotage activities in favor of the patriots [i.e., the Resistance]."[2] This episode introduces us to the routine nature of the genocide of the Jews at the hands of the Italians, including subsequent erasure of all responsibility and absolution of all guilt in addition to credit awarded for anti-Fascist activities. This story also reveals brief flashes of light in those dark months. They are seen in the attempts to protect or save victims, as in the case of the concierges who tried to save Emma. And they are visible in the partial acts of attrition or the attempts to derail the pursuit of the Jews, as in the case of the concierges and, according to their statements, one of the agents.

Over the years, historians have developed a far more subtle and complex approach to their interpretation of the paths that led to the destruction of the European

Jews. They no longer envision the process as the product of the mind of a cruel dictator and his willing henchmen, developing linearly by means of a predetermined persecutory escalation, thanks to relentless, ideologically motivated executioners. Nor do they ascribe it to an anonymous and unstoppable bureaucratic mechanism, following a plan of extermination whose every detail had been established from the very beginning. That which we call Holocaust or Shoah was produced during the course of World War II and was the result of a variety of factors, actions, and a multitude of circumstances. The war context played a decisive role as did the diverse initiatives and operations that were put into place by the Nazi regime. Moreover, with the growing expansion of Nazism in Europe, the collaborationist governments and regimes became persecutors in their own right—in some cases having already been so for some time. They acted from the periphery toward the center, or from the bottom up the ladders of the administrative, political, and military hierarchies of the countries involved in the extermination. Vast sectors of European society therefore played a fundamental role by collaborating: from the bureaucracies to the economy, from services to infrastructure, men and women of every nationality—thousands of ordinary citizens—participated in arrests, plunder, deportation, and extermination. Placing the Holocaust in a comparative perspective within the study of genocide also permits us to intensify and reshape the analysis of the individual behavior of the executioners. Together with the ideologically motivated persecutors, and alongside the bureaucrats carrying out every type of order, we now focus on a variety of figures with different functions and degrees of responsibility, intertwined in a tangle of organizational roles, competition, imitation, and the pursuit of profit. These factors could influence alone or in concert with other factors such as obedience, compliance, and allegiance, as well as a desire for satisfaction, reward, or success in a context in which ideological motivations could just as easily be absent or minimal. It is rarely possible to completely isolate these different factors. They should be viewed as a "series of incremental and not always intentional shifts" that create a situation in which organization, obedience to orders, pressure from superiors and peers, and imitation and emulation—or, again, the desire for gain—make "active participation" in genocide "more easily self-justified."[3] Moreover, as historian Raul Hilberg and sociologist Zygmunt Bauman have underscored, the subdivision or parceling of functions and the distance from the final outcome of the extermination facilitated the implementation of the various procedures and phases of genocide up to its extreme conclusions.[4] Finally, it has been remarked that "in a civil war [the backdrop to the Holocaust in Italy between 1943 and 1945] violence is never purely instrumental. It takes on a strong symbolic dimension, feeds on itself and acquires its own dynamic, eventually becoming an end in itself."[5]

The Roman episode described at the start of this chapter reminds us, among other things, that over six hundred Roman Jews were arrested in the weeks and months after the infamous Nazi roundup of October 16, 1943. These arrests were mainly carried out by Italian police and Fascists, in myriad individual episodes. Awareness and records of these incidents have been partially obscured by that symbolic date, which has become the most notorious anti-Jewish action carried out by the Germans in Italy.[6] This particular episode in Rome can best be examined by asking ourselves specific questions about the situation and about the motivations of the executioners, which apply to this occasion as well as to a multitude of similar instances.[7] They are outlined below in the form of interpretative hypotheses postulated by the historian. In the majority of cases—both here and later on in my reconstruction—they will remain mere hypotheses, questions lacking definitive answers, tentative queries with verbs used in the conditional tense.

As far as we can determine, the police commissioner who arrested Enrica Calò and her family does not seem to have been an executioner ideologically motivated by antisemitism. He appears more like someone obeying orders: orders that he claims to have otherwise frequently ignored in his work with the Resistance. But by asking further questions relating to the actor's motivation, even the mere execution of orders can be examined with more focus and in greater depth. Were these orders carried out with conviction, even if just the conviction that orders simply must be carried out? Or were they carried out owing to pressure from superiors or peers? Are we observing, therefore, bureaucratic routine? Or were those orders carried out and those arrests made because of the influence of an ideologically conditioned context or as a result of a kind of resignation about a fate that was already sealed? Was this done with the awareness of what fate awaited the victims or without knowing and without asking, or rather ignoring and avoiding the question?[8] The search and arrests were the apparent product of an informer's tip. Was the informer someone who knew

Enrica and her family? Was he or she an acquaintance of the concierges with some reason to resent them? Or motivated by the promise of a reward for notifying the police? Or inspired by anti-Jewish sentiments and the desire to persecute Jewish fellow citizens? The evidence given by the witnesses suggests that the police commissioner seemed particularly determined to arrest the entire family, including the minors who had attempted to escape: Did he always follow his orders so painstakingly or was he just playing the part of the dutiful agent for the benefit of his superiors? Maybe on that particular day he had needed or wanted to demonstrate relentless resolve to cover up or deflect attention from other unsuccessful arrests. Maybe he had taken advantage of a tip concerning a large group of people that included children and the elderly to prove his commitment was free of qualms, to show that he would let nothing and no one stop him from doing his job. It is possible that Enrica and her family were sacrificed because of this personal need—because they simply represented an opportunity for cover. These questions are destined to remain unanswered.

Let us reflect on another episode. During the night of February 3, 1944, into the early morning of the following day, Pietro Koch led a raid on St. Paul's Basilica with the approval and support of the chief of police of Rome, Pietro Caruso. Yet again the Italian police played a key role, but this time they were bolstered by operations led by the Fascist elements in their ranks. In his report to the national chief of police, Tullio Tamburini, Koch described the assault as follows: "There were 80 uniformed agents from Public Security with 5 officers and 10 non-commissioned officers, 18 plainclothes police under the

command of Lieutenant Tela as well as two commissioners from Public Security, all equipped with 8 vehicles
under my direct command." Because the basilica was Vatican sovereign territory, the operation had to be carried
out with the utmost care, yet apparently Koch had been
given a free hand by those at the highest levels: "During
a meeting in an office at the police headquarters and in
the presence of the [Roman] police chief himself I gave
everyone precise instructions and, given the immense importance of the venue, strict orders regarding the treatment of the clergy." Things happened very fast: "In just
a few minutes, and in almost complete silence, the huge
complex and [Vatican] guardhouses were under our control. While groups of three or four police began a room-
by-room search of the premises [. . .]." The raid led to
the arrest of a general and four other high-ranking army
officers, two policemen, forty-eight draft-dodging young
men, and nine Jews. Koch concluded his report by describing his men as "perfect, tireless, true bloodhounds."

A twenty-five-year-old salesman from Abruzzo with a
criminal record, Pietro Koch began his militant career
in the RSI in Florence under the command of the Fascist Mario Carità. In January 1944, he created a special
police unit in Rome with the authorization and possibly
even the support of the aforementioned national chief of
police, Tamburini. He was subsequently enrolled in the
police corps as auxiliary commissioner and finally as auxiliary police chief. Many of the men under his command
were Tuscans from the infamous Carità paramilitary unit
or from the 92nd Legion of the Milizia volontaria di
sicurezza nazionale (Voluntary Militia for National Security [MVSN]—the military arm of the Fascist party).

Aged between twenty and twenty-five, they mainly wore plainclothes and were all armed, although only one of them was an actual policeman. The Koch gang, like the Carità gang, mainly hunted down anti-Fascists, *badogliani* (Italian soldiers who had remained faithful to General Badoglio, who had become prime minister in the summer of 1943 after Mussolini's toppling), and draft dodgers. They considered Jews a collateral target: in fact, they accounted for only 15 of the more than 600 arrests during the entire Salò period.[9] The gang members were a mixture of regular police and men motivated by ideology—though not necessarily by antisemitism—and certainly eager to make a profit or even just to use their weapons (as in the case of the Fascists associated with Koch). The primary motivation behind this particular episode may have been the wish to capture soldiers who had "betrayed" the cause or had avoided the draft. The apprehension of Jews during the operation may have represented a kind of additional trophy. It is also possible that the tips about the hideout in St. Paul's Basilica had made specific mention of the Jews who were sheltered there. According to Koch, the Fascist promoted to auxiliary police chief, he and his men hunted like "bloodhounds," and they may have intended to catch several types of prey from the very start. They made no distinction among their victims: they were all traitors or enemies of Fascism, enemies of the nation. The majority of the policemen, on the other hand, were merely obeying orders. It is possible that they were given the opportunity to withdraw from such a delicate operation, with some accepting the offer, fearing or disapproving of an invasion of Church territory. Others may not have wished or dared to refuse the chief's orders, or felt competition and pressure from their peers, or simply acted because those were their orders: the routine work of capturing criminals, draft dodgers, *badogliani*, or Jews—all of them considered dangerous outlaws. In February 1944, while enacting Tamburini's order to break up the Italian Jewish communities and seize their property, Caruso, Rome's chief of police, defined the Jewish community as being "at the current time an association representing a threat to public order and safety, and in conflict with the political systems of the State."[10]

Historian Bruno Maida has remarked that "when reading the stories of every single Jew who, from December 8, 1943 onward, had to invent a strategy to save himself, it becomes clear that an equal number of Italians must have been involved in their capture in one way or another—either as accomplices or as silent spectators."[11] And the most common and tragic form of complicity was informing. This phenomenon played a key role in the Republic of Salò both in the civil war, between the Fascists and the anti-Fascist partisans or other "traitors," and in the genocide of the Jews. In the case of the Jews, informing was rife not only in most Italian towns but also on the border between Italy and Switzerland, which, if they could successfully cross it, should have guaranteed safety to persecuted fugitives.

Let us consider some other episodes. Between December 1943 and January 1944, a couple were working as informers at Lake Maggiore in the Intra region. The woman would identify and ensnare fleeing Jews willing to pay large sums of money to cross the border, and the man would offer to be their guide on the perilous foot journey to Switzerland, which involved facing various dangers, logistical difficulties, and narrow, twisting paths. The postwar court records inform us that on December 6, 1943, using the ruse just described, the couple betrayed both Edoardo Orefice and Giorgio and Jole Goldschmiedt, pocketing the money given to them by the fugitives to help them in their flight, and, most likely, the bounty as well. They used the same method to the detriment of Carlo Bassi and his mother. On January 9, 1944, the woman obtained 45,000 lire from Bassi in exchange for the promise of supplying him with a guide. Shortly after picking up the fugitives in his car and heading for the border, the guide "blew his horn insistently." The car was flagged down by Fascist guards who took mother and son to the local Fascist commissioner in Intra. At that point the guide "declared himself to be a Republican [Fascist] and accused Bassi and his mother of being Jews who were attempting to expatriate. The unfortunate pair was stripped of all their money and their suitcases." Carlo Bassi was frisked and stripped of the gold and jewelry on his person "totaling approximately 400,000 lire." After about a week of detainment in the local prisons of Varese, for reasons that are not clear, the Fascist commissioner released Carlo and his mother: Was this executioner coming to his senses or repenting of his actions? He would even return their seized valuables to them after the war was over. The woman was brought to trial for collaborationism by the heirs of the victims but only spent a brief period in preventive detention in 1945; a series of appeals, requests for pardons, deferments for reasons of ill health, and evidence given in her defense by a Jewess and partisan woman who had received her assistance led to her sentence being completely annulled in December 1953.[12]

In this case we find ourselves in the presence of habitual informers (which does not exclude isolated acts of help or mercy) whose desire for profit became a financial scheme and an unrestrained motivation for criminal conduct. At the same time, we cannot ignore the fact that the treacherous driver had made a declaration of political allegiance to the victims—presenting himself as a Republican Fascist—and had handed the Jews over to other equally political Fascists rather than to the police or military authorities. In many other, if not the majority of, cases, they were not habitual informers, nor were they guided by political motives, although "ordinary" informers looking to make a quick buck may have given such motives to support, legitimize, or justify such behavior in their own consciences. Most instances of informing were in fact motivated by a vast variety of reasons ranging from resentment to quarrels, from personal vendettas to a desire for profit. In fact, there was an official bounty system with rewards offered according to fixed rates for anyone who turned in a Jew. Informing, after all, had been strongly incentivized during the twenty-year period of Fascism and became widespread during the years of the regime, which was largely founded on suspicion, the threat of being reported, and the fear of betrayal.[13] From 1943 to 1945, in a context of civil war—a war in which everyone was against everyone else and the enemy could be lurking anywhere—and of genocide, in which enemies were not just enemies of a political faction but of the entire nation, and therefore destined to be deported and ultimately eliminated, informing was not just a socially accepted practice but virtually an existential strategy.

In the daily routine of events, normality, already turned upside down by the world war, by civil war, and finally by genocide, would be shattered by an initial act of violence that would unleash a chain of actions whose ultimate consequences were not yet known to all but that were part of a political plan with a persecutory intent. And the aforementioned social legitimization meant that the first stirrings of genocide might take place on a tram. In Milan in December 1944, two Jewish women who had thus far escaped arrest suddenly found the search closing in on them—although they did not immediately realize that this was the case—when one of their husbands was arrested. One day, the tenant of the apartment let by one of their families before going into hiding invited them over with an offer of help. Afterward, he chatted with them briefly on the street before offering them a cigarette and then disappearing. Only later did they realize that this must have been a prearranged signal intended to alert someone to their presence. The two women were immediately approached by plainclothesmen who took them to an apartment for questioning in order to obtain the names and addresses of other Jews. They were then arrested and taken by tram to the San Vittore prison.[14] The tram crossing the city to take the two women accompanied by their plainclothes executioners toward their fate of suffering and persecution (even though in this particular case both women would survive the war) both literally and figuratively represents the reality of informing and arrests in the daily life of the Italian people from 1943 to 1945. Whether for the profit of those doing the reporting or in obedience to orders from superiors, victims were identified, arrested, and deported in clear view of ordinary people, transformed from fellow citizens into "enemies" by the political and ideological context and the resulting laws. What did the people around them think? It's hard to say, and their disapproval certainly cannot be excluded: they would undoubtedly have realized that this was a dangerous state of affairs and that these were rash, violent acts. The tram driver may not have realized what was going on, or he may have recognized the thugs from the police headquarters. Other passengers probably noticed that the two women were traveling under close guard, against their will, carefully watched and controlled and forced to get off at the stop right in front of the San Vittore prison. But they lowered their gaze or turned away, pretending not to understand: war desensitizes people to everything. Still others may have watched the scene frozen with fear, while someone else may have even quietly muttered his approval.

Precedents, Institutions, Actors

If we consider a longer-term institutional perspective in addition to these circumstantial conditions, we could find that the genocidal turn of events in the fall of 1943 was also the result of an escalation process that had begun three years earlier, before the birth of the RSI. Upon Italy's entry into the world conflict, the Fascists undertook to intern Jews who were considered "dangerous" or who were foreigners. The project was launched with the following communication, dated May 26, 1940, from Undersecretary of the Interior Guido Buffarini Guidi to Bocchini, the national chief of police: "The Duce asks that concentration camps also be prepared for Jews, in case of war." The next day, Bocchini gave the prefects the following order: "In case of an emergency, in addition to the foreign Jews whom, per previous memoranda, it will be necessary to intern, it may also become necessary to intern, removing them from their usual residences, those Italian Jews who represent substantive danger." He went on to specify: "You are requested to draw up the related lists, which must be ready by June 10."[15] In another communication, probably sent to the prefects in the second half of June 1940, Bocchini wrote: "As soon as there is room in the prisons [. . .] you shall proceed with the search for foreign Jews belonging to states with racial policies. In order to protect public order, the aforementioned undesirables, filled with hate for totalitarian regimes and capable of any and all harmful action, must be removed from circulation forthwith. Therefore, German Jews, former Czechoslovakians, Poles, and stateless persons from 18 to 60 years of age must be arrested." Six months later Buffarini Guidi again emphasized the need to expedite the rate at which "elements whose feelings and conduct give the most cause for suspicion" were being sent to camps. The undersecretary noted in fact that "once again [the Jews had] demonstrated their obtuse lack of understanding with regard to current political and historic events, proving themselves to be constitutionally opposed to every national sentiment."[16] These measures were effectively realized against foreign Jews, while in the summer of 1942 large numbers of Italian Jews were sent to do forced labor, a measure that reflected the racial basis of their exploitation. A year later—only a few weeks before the fall of Mussolini's regime in July 1943— the Ministry of Corporations and the General Administrations for Demography and Race and Public Safety approved the orders for the "establishment of labor camps for citizens of the Jewish race" both Italian and foreign between eighteen and thirty-six years of age. Although preparations were interrupted by the fall of Mussolini, this measure represented a further phase of anti-Jewish action when compared to the anti-Jewish persecutory action of Fascism enforced in 1938.[17]

Thus we see that the provisions for arresting Jews ordered at the end of November 1943 by the Italian Social Republic found, in fact, certain precedents in the measures for internment from the early years of the war and in those issued in the last weeks of the regime before Mussolini's fall. These precedents should be added to the ideological and propagandistic premises established by the racist shift of 1938—which included bureaucratic and administrative measures such as compiling lists of citizens belonging to the "Jewish race."

These provisions already contemplated the use of concentration camps and the segregation of "dangerous" Jews for reasons of public security or of physically able Jews for exploitation through forced labor, although this was only applied to foreign Jews. After the armistice of September 8, 1943, there was a new harshening of anti-Jewish measures driven and sometimes even initiated by the lower ranks of the party hierarchy—and from the periphery toward the center of political and administrative power. As we shall see, new measures against Jews were being invoked by the base of the reborn Fascist party from September 1943 onward, and in October, calls from the Fascist press began to demand a definitive "solution" to the problem.

The Jews could no longer expect "any mercy from us," thundered the extremist paper *Il Regime fascista* on October 4, 1943, while the daily *Popolo di Alessandria* made the following demands: "Let us confiscate *all* their property [. . .], burn out their lairs, [. . .] drive them from the country, *now!*"[18] At the beginning of November, both local and national newspapers announced that the Ministry of the Interior was "studying measures concerning the Jewish question" that would follow "the guidelines set by the [Nazi] Nuremberg laws": not just confiscations and economic restrictions but also—reflecting the wishes of *Il Regime fascista*—a "clear-cut racial discrimination."[19] By the middle of the month the Jewish question was numbered among the key concerns of Republican Fascism by the Verona Congress. As party secretary Alessandro Pavolini read out his report to the congress he was repeatedly interrupted by calls for harsher measures: "As you know, we are currently working on provisions for the confiscation of Jewish property [*from the audience: 'About time,' 'That's right,' expressions of approval*]. Without indulging in rhetoric, this [wealth] represents blood sucked from the people [*from the audience: 'Watch out for transfers of Jewish property to Italians,' 'How long will it be until you start transferring the Jews?' 'This is not enough, not enough.'*]. There are Jews who deserve . . . [*interruptions: 'All,' 'All,' 'Of course'*] Of course they are foreigners who belong to an enemy nation [*from the audience: 'Well said,' 'Right,' 'That is certain'*] and they are enemies!"[20] On the Jewish question, the temperature of the reborn Fascist party had clearly reached a feverish level. It was on the lookout for scapegoats, on the hunt for traitors, and aiming to radicalize the measures introduced by the regime in 1938 but that many claimed had never been enacted with sufficient firmness, especially on an economic level. The last of Pavolini's remarks on the Jews referred to point 7 of the manifesto approved by the Verona Congress as part of the principles guiding the "constitutional and internal matters" of the new Italian Social Republic. It seems that immediately after the Verona Congress a meeting was held in Florence between the minister of the interior, Guido Buffarini Guidi, and the prefects of the RSI. During that meeting he outlined the coming measures for them. They were no longer limited to the seizure of Jewish property but probably already included the arrest of Jews. Shortly afterward, the meeting was mentioned by Ercolani, the prefect of Grosseto, who was—as we shall see—the first prefect to enact measures for arresting Jews in his province. And he must have done this by no later than mid-November 1943 given that on November 18 he was praised by the Germans for having given the "order to intern all the Jews."[21]

The RSI had various institutions and "actors of violence" (as they have been described in a recent study): "the traditional State apparatuses"; the Fascist party, which claimed a "monopoly in the use of violence"; the Voluntary Militia for National Security (MVSN), which later became the National Republican Guard (GNR) and also included the *carabinieri* (the military police); and other armed corps, acting independently or under German orders, with a kind of "license to abuse their power."[22] All these bodies were involved in the Italian phase of the genocide of the Jews, albeit in varying ways and with varying functions and degrees of responsibility depending on the precise moment, geographic context, and specific episode. The police forces and state apparatuses were at the top of the chain of command responsible for executing arrest and deportation orders. Yet they were frequently supported—and occasionally replaced—by the MVSN and then by the GNR, by elements of the party, by units or individuals at the service of the Germans, or by autonomous groups. In the context of ongoing conflict and war these entities were not steady and structured in how they carried out arrests. Sometimes they were strongly driven in their work, other times not. They were all vested with different powers and varying levels of freedom to act on those powers. The competition between these bodies and their leadership at both the local and national levels caused Buffarini Guidi to complain in June 1944 that "in Italy everyone is making arrests and we need to put a stop to this noxious lawlessness."[23] Along with the uninterrupted work of the police forces, similar tasks related to identifying and combating internal political enemies from the late fall of 1943 to August 1944 were also attributed to the MVSN, which was dependent on the prefects. In the summer of 1944, the GNR, which had now combined police duties with its original ideological-political inspiration, became part of the national Republican Army. In the meantime the Brigate Nere (Black Brigades), the armed branch of the Fascist party, had been established in June 1944. In December 1944 there was an overhaul of the entire Republican police and its political offices, including the border, railway, highway, port, and post and telegraph police bodies, and at least the first three were frequently involved in anti-Jewish persecution. Still in January 1945, when the RSI was nearing its end, renewed investigatory and political functions were assigned to the GNR, while military and repressive actions were allocated to the Brigate Nere.[24] It has furthermore been noted that in this rapid and sometimes confused succession of organizational arrangements, the offices and bodies of the Ministry of the Interior sought to reclaim their traditional monopoly in the management of public order in addition to "social and moral order," while adopting a moderating function with regard to both the party and the GNR. The various departments in the Ministry of the Interior therefore found themselves having to mediate between other groups or structures that had taken on policing functions: they often did so by "making legal what was illegal." Moreover, the ministry was the most willing of the collaborators in meeting the demands of the German occupiers even with regard to anti-Jewish persecution.[25] The party, for its part, had continued developing a paramilitary, totalitarian approach since the final years of the regime, causing it to consider its adversaries "enemies to be eliminated or humiliated."[26] In the clash of the civil war, this "approach" transformed into a fratricidal war without limits, consummately intensifying the contrast and the conflict between "us" and "them."

Minister Buffarini Guidi issued the police order for the general arrest of Jews present on Italian soil on November 30, 1943. A German-Italian agreement was probably reached on that date or, more likely, between December 1943 and January 1944, either immediately before or simultaneously with the provision issued for the confiscation of the already seized Jewish property on January 4, 1944. That measure was followed by one for the dissolution of Jewish communities and confiscation of their holdings on January 28, 1944. According to historian Michele Sarfatti, the Third Reich and the RSI had come "to an agreement over the delivery to the Germans and the subsequent deportation (and murder) of the Jews arrested by the Italians."[27] Sarfatti dates this agreement between December 14, 1943, and February 6, 1944, although local agreements would already have been in place with the Germans at least as far as arrest procedures were concerned, since many of the first arrest warrants transmitted were already referring to them in early December.

A Ministry of the Interior memorandum dated December 27, 1943, documents the search for a suitable site for a second national concentration camp in addition to the one at Fossoli (near the city of Modena)—the main transit camp for Jews deported from Italy—with a capacity large enough for "several thousand Jews and [...] all the suspicious elements already detained or yet to be detained,"[28] and there are even suggestions that the Italians planned to create a "vast concentration system with a network of forced labor camps."[29] Even the mere internment of Italian Jews in such camps—pretending for a moment that they were not to be deported and exterminated by the Germans—would have most likely led in the long run to genocidal consequences for Italy's Jewry at the hands of Italians. There would have been high death tolls due to the poor living conditions—as had been the case in the extreme conditions of the prison camps of the Italian colonial occupation of Libya in the 1930s and during the Italian wartime occupation of Slovenia and Croatia. In fact, in the counterfactual hypothesis that the project of the Nazi "Final Solution" had not existed—the Jews in the territories under Fascist control, even within the national borders of Italy, may nevertheless have found themselves in a situation of subordination, submission, and, in a period of war, detention: again, potentially ending in genocide. We may extrapolate this on the basis of the policies for Italian occupation, territorial control, or detention of population segments or groups in colonial or war contexts, along with Fascist Italy's general direction and plans in the struggle for the "new Mediterranean order"[30] (and on the basis of the actual projects for the detention and concentration in Italy of the "dangerous" Jews described above).

Be that as it may, the Italian Fascists and police forces provided crucial help for the realization of the Nazi project to exterminate the Jews, so much so that in Italy, as elsewhere in Europe, it would not have reached the scale it did without their collaboration. In a note to Minister Ribbentrop at the start of the deportations in December 1943, a German diplomatic counselor informed him that "with the forces at our disposal in Italy, it is impossible to comb through all the towns from smallest to largest."[31] It is valid to believe—in fact it is virtually always attested—that the overwhelming majority of arrests made by the Germans, including the notorious roundup of October 16, 1943, in Rome, received organizational support from the Italians. If nothing else, these would not have been possible without the essential lists of the names of Jews living in every city and town. Frequently such support involved the physical presence and direct collaboration or action of Italian forces working alongside the German military.

The Germans in Italy, the Camp at Fossoli, and the Final Massacres

Setting up the German army and police involved the coordination of arrests and deportations by Department IV-B4 of the Security Police (SiPo), headed in Berlin by Adolf Eichmann and represented in Verona, Italy, initially by SS captain Theodor Dannecker, followed by Friedrich Bosshamer from the end of January 1944 onward.[32] Dannecker was personally responsible for coordinating the arrests of Italian Jews in the fall of 1943, beginning with the Roman roundup of October 16, for which he received logistical support from Rome's police headquarters. In September, the head of the Race Department of the Italian police in Rome had informed the Roman Jewish community of SS Major Kappler's demand for its gold in exchange for its freedom (a promise unfulfilled by the Germans).[33] In early November 1943, Dannecker and his men were additionally in charge of roundups in Florence, Siena, Bologna, and Montecatini. A month later, Dannecker probably oversaw the first deportation transport, which left Milan for Auschwitz on December 6, 1943.[34]

Both Dannecker and, at a higher level, ambassador Rudolf Rahn, the Reich's political and diplomatic representative in Italy, had previously served in Paris: Rahn was in the special services under Otto Abetz, German

ambassador in France, while Dannecker was in charge
of organizing the arrest and deportation of the Jews in
the French capital between 1940 and 1942.[35] The previous experiences of these two men suggest that the Germans had considered transforming the RSI into a sort
of Vichy (the collaborationist government of France),
that is, a "half allied, half satellite," government. It has,
however, been pointed out that unlike Vichy, where the
French initially handed over only foreign Jews, and where,
after the German occupation, a bureaucratic administrative system had to be created in order to identify and
create files on the Jewish victims, the Fascists handed over
Italian Jews right from the start—without distinguishing
between their treatment and that of foreign Jews (unlike
in France). This was due to the fact that the Fascist administrative and propagandistic bureaucracy had been
in place in Italy since 1938, facilitating a sort of natural
development of Italian racial policy. In Italy, therefore,
it was possible for the Germans to hit the ground running: by that time (fall 1943) the Shoah had already been
underway for some time in eastern Europe.[36] In mid-
December 1943, German foreign minister Ribbentrop
asked Ambassador Rahn to inform the Fascist government, which had taken the initiative and given the order
for the arrest of the Jews a couple of weeks earlier, of
the "German government's satisfaction with the [Italian
government's] recognition of the need based on security reasons to intern all of Italy's Jews in concentration
camps." Rahn was to invite the Italians to intensify this
procedure "in the interests," claimed the note, "of protect-
ing the area of operations [in north-central Italy] from
undesirables."[37]

From February 1944 onward, German operations for the "Final Solution" in Italy were coordinated by Bosshamer from the Verona headquarters through the advanced units (or smaller peripheral units) of the German army commissariats stationed in the main towns in north-central Italy. At that time, even the jurisdiction and management of the Fossoli camp, from which Jewish prisoners were periodically deported to Auschwitz via Verona, also passed into German hands. In August 1944, Fossoli was abandoned following the Allied advance in central Italy, and the main German transit camp became Gries, near Bolzano. From September 1943 onward, the Operational Zones of the Adriatic Littoral (Adriatisches Küstenland: from Udine to Ljubljana) and of the Alpine Foothills (Alpenvorland: from Bolzano to Belluno) were occupied and administered directly by Germany, through two *Gauleiter* (high commissioners) answering to Hitler. The Adriatisches Küstenland was also home to the only concentration and extermination camp on Italian soil: the German-run former rice mill known as the Risiera di San Sabba in Trieste.[38] This camp, though established and run by the Germans, could not have operated without local Italian support.

Most of the Italian Jews arrested outside these two zones under direct German control traveled instead via the Fossoli camp, which was run exclusively by Italian forces from December 1943 to February 1944. Established in the spring of 1942 as a prisoner-of-war camp on farmland about a kilometer from Fossoli and five kilometers from the center of Carpi, it began operating as a "*Campo concentramento ebrei*," or Jewish concentration camp, on December 5, 1943.[39] A few days earlier, after receiving orders from his superiors, the prefect of Modena had invited the Carpi municipality to make arrangements with the local police headquarters to carry out the urgent "installation work" necessary to "set up a concentration camp for the Jews." This work, which continued until the closure of the camp in August 1944, involved expanding existing facilities to create a new camp and was carried out by a local cooperative of masons, concrete finishers, and artisans. The camp was under the jurisdiction of the Italian police who answered to the prefect of Modena, who was first the adjunct vice-commissioner, Domenico Avitabile, and was later replaced by commissioner Mario Tagliatela. A study commissioned by the Comitato Ricerche Deportati Ebrei (Research Committee on Jewish Deportees) in the summer of 1945 in cooperation with the Office of the Prime Minister of Italy described Avitabile, who was still at large in Milan at the time, as a "fanatical Republican Fascist. A crude, violent man, he ill-treated all the detainees, whether Jewish or political prisoners." The report recalled that Tagliatela was "tried and condemned for his Nazi-Fascist activities" and that he "would free detainees in exchange for large sums of money."[40]

The choice of Fossoli as the location for a national transit camp that integrated the provincial camps may have already been made with the agreement of the German authorities. Historian Liliana Picciotto believes, moreover, that right from the start there must have been a political accord between the Italians and Germans with regard to the first phase of the persecutions: "The Italian police would be in charge of tracking down Jews, their arrest and internment at Fossoli, and the Germans were to be responsible for their subsequent deportation."[41] In the beginning the task of guarding the camp fell entirely to the Italians. It involved police, *carabinieri*, and members of the MVSN, thus combining police and political units. A letter from the camp superintendent to the chief of police in Modena stated that in mid-February 1944, the initial staff of just thirty *carabinieri* was joined by sixty men from the GNR and an additional reinforcement of *carabinieri* to carry out daily shifts.[42]

It seems that conditions in the camp were initially acceptable, and prisoners were directly involved in various areas of its internal organization, including the distribution of food, education, leisure activities, and a legal office. A letter dated February 1944, signed by a group of prisoners including the rabbis of the cities of Modena and Gorizia, and addressed to the bishop of Carpi and the archbishop of Modena, appealed for "spiritual and material support, and help for our miserable conditions" and the "aid that the elderly, women, children, and the ill implore from human solidarity."[43] Although the food rations were scarce, inmates could pool their money to buy supplies in Carpi. According to the above-mentioned report to the Research Committee on Jewish Deportees, a *carabiniere* from Forlì stationed at the camp was willing to "do certain favors for the inmates always in exchange for considerable sums of money."[44] It was theoretically possible for the prisoners to leave the camp briefly for pressing or serious reasons. In fact, just a few days before being deported from Fossoli, Luciana Nissim received a letter permitting her to take her medical board exams. The prefect of Turin had sent a letter to the Ministry of the Interior authorizing her attendance at the request of the camp management;[45] this suggests that peripheral bodies—along with the camp management—envisaged a relatively long period of detention in the camp. In a letter sent to the national police chief on January 14, 1944, the Modena chief of police states that on that date "around 500 Jews" were being held in the Fossoli camp, which is described as "still under construction." During that winter around 1,200 detainees—Italian and foreign civilians—arrived in another section of the camp, followed by 170-190 political prisoners. With the exception of the Jews of "mixed" race, who were detained for longer periods, the prisoners were replaced by others following deportation at regular intervals to various camps in Germany and Poland, with the Jews being sent to the extermination camp at Auschwitz.[46]

Although the camp came under the direct jurisdiction of the German authorities in March 1944, the support for the daily operation of the camp—guarding it and furnishing its provisions—remained in Italian hands. And for the entire length of the operation of the camp, Italians provided the means of transportation that deported prisoners. The buses that brought them to the train station at Carpi and the convoys of ten freight cars supplied by the Italian State and Rail company were all Italian run, and an Italian engineer drove the train, at least as far as the Italian border. The supplier of the food provisions for the journey was also Italian. The train was escorted by Germans, but on occasion it was guarded by *carabinieri* at the departure station.[47] Every convoy transported 500 to 600 prisoners, cramming 50 into each of the ten freight cars with only a bucket for their bodily needs.[48] There are many horrifying accounts of these journeys toward death.

Italian Jews were not always exterminated outside of Italy after being deported. At the beginning of the civil war in the fall of 1943, Jews were killed by German soldiers in several massacres in northern Italy, and during the final months of the RSI (1945) small groups of Jews were murdered on Italian soil by Germans with Italian help or by Italians alone. Fascist GNR militia also provided support for a massacre of mainly Jewish victims by the SS in the Emilia region. On September 5, 1944, seventeen prisoners were killed, including eleven Jews, in the Casermette quarter near the airport of Forlì. On September 17, seven women (mothers, wives, and sisters of the aforementioned prisoners) were promised their freedom and told that they were being released from the local prisons before being shot: in the meantime the area was being patrolled by armed GNR. On April 25, 1945—or possibly on the following day—members of the Fascist Black Brigades retreating from Cuneo ordered that the local police hand over six foreign Jews accused of collaborating with the partisans and then shot them. Shortly before, they had likewise executed the commander of the local Garibaldi Brigade (i.e., Communist) partisans on the banks of the river Stura.[49] Even in the days of the Liberation, until the final moments, rather than slowing, this bloodbath inside Italy's borders actually intensified.

Overall from 1943 to 1945, 8,869 Jews living on Italian soil (according to the borders of the period, including the Italian territories in the Dodecannese islands of Greece)[50] were deported. That number amounts to about 19 percent of the 47,000 Jews recorded in the racist census of 1938.[51] Of them, 6,746 were deported from Italy and 303 died in Italy in massacres, in individual murders, or from other causes. Italians participated in or were responsible for just under half of the total Jewish arrests. This amounted to 2,210 arrests, 1,898 of which were made by Italians acting alone, and 312 were made by Italians acting together with Germans. Over half of the remaining total, or 2,489 arrests, were carried out by Germans. However, we must bear in mind that arrests by Germans were always carried out with the help of information and organizational support from the Italians, or at least in the presence of some of them. Moreover, data on those responsible for making the arrests need to be refined and studied in the light of local research.[52] In fact, 2,314 of the total number of arrests were carried out by persons still unknown. In chronological terms, a very significant number of arrests were made in the fall of 1943, even before the Italian order of arrest of November 30; the number remained high between February and March 1944 with an average of over 400 arrests per month; it peaked for the final time in August 1944 and then decreased in the early months of 1945. In geographical terms, the number of arrests per city is obviously linked to demographics (the cities with the largest Jewish populations were Rome, Trieste, Milan, Florence, Venice, and Turin), as well as to the vicinity of the border, which saw large numbers of foreign Jews pouring into the nearest Italian towns from abroad (as was the case in Cuneo and the surrounding province) or moving to these towns on their flight to safety abroad (for example, in the areas of Varese and Como). There were also numerous small villages where Jews had gone into hiding before being captured or where they had lived undisturbed for long periods of time. The great majority of deportees from Italy were sent to Auschwitz, followed by Bergen-Belsen and Ravensbrück, while smaller numbers of prisoners were sent to other camps.

Three

The Beginning of the Persecutions

Even before the official Italian order to arrest Jews was issued at the end of November 1943, some prefects—in response to pressure from fringe segments of the reborn Fascism—took it upon themselves to initiate arrests. On September 13, in Rome, the chief of police had given orders to arrest the most "fanatical Communists," "troublemakers in general," "including Jews dangerous to public order."[1] In October, calls for arrests were made by the party's base: in Padua, the Ettore Muti paramilitary squad demanded the "internment of all Jews," while in Rome the assembly of the Republican Fascist Party asked that "all Jews be immediately contained in concentration camps."[2] At the end of October, the newspaper *Il Popolo di Alessandria* thundered: "Away with all the Jews of Italy! Including the 'exonerated'![3] Immediate confiscation of their property! Immediate arrest of all of their front men! We are still in time but we need to act, act, act!"[4] In mid-November, in Ferrara, there was a punitive raid to avenge the death of the local party secretary, Igino Ghisellini, which resulted in the executions of eleven civilians. The victims included two Jews, in addition to anti-Fascists,

members of the regime who had fallen from favor, and ordinary citizens. The raid was meant as an act of vendetta
against Fascism's "traitors."[5] But it was now up to prefects
and police commissioners to take action.

Between October and early November, prefectures and
police headquarters, and, occasionally, once more, members of the reborn Fascist party, offered their support for
the first roundups of Jews by the Germans. This was certainly the case in Rome. The preparations for the arrest of
over a thousand Roman Jews on October 16, 1943, were
based on the lists of names supplied by Demorazza (the
Office for Racial Affairs of the Italian Ministry of the
Interior) and possibly also by the Roman Fascist Federation. As we shall see, this was also the case in Florence,
where the local Fascists acted as guides for the Germans
who were conducting the arrests in the city. In the province of Piacenza, the chief of police ordered Jews to remain confined "in the communes where they presently
reside" (November 19); in Rieti, the prefect asked for authorization to arrest nine Jews already interned in that
province (November 25).[6] Elsewhere steps were taken
to organize and update the lists of Jews that had been
compiled since the racist census of 1938. At the end of
the month, the microphones of Radio Roma expressed
the explicit hope that the "Jews be burnt, one by one,
and their ashes scattered in the wind."[7]

The earliest, most concrete initiative was carried out
by the prefect of Grosseto, Alceo Ercolani, a former army
officer from Viterbo who had also moved up through the
ranks of the Fascist party; he was an authoritarian, violent man perhaps motivated more by his bureaucratic,
repressive zeal than by specific anti-Jewish intentions.[8]

On November 25, Ercolani made an announcement to the Directorate General of Public Security, stating that "all Italian Jews of the Province of Grosseto, even if they have been exonerated, will be interned." He went on to specify that a "concentration camp" at Roccatederighi (a small town near Grosseto) would begin operations on November 28. This measure had been preceded earlier that month by the prefectorial request to carry out a census of residences and properties and to draw up lists of the members of Jewish families. Simultaneously initiatives were launched for the seizure of farm holdings and financial holdings belonging to Jews. When a local citizen asked for further details of the procedures taking place, Ercolani replied, "In any business where there is a single Jew [. . .] steps must be taken to confiscate it," claiming that the initiative was being carried out in response to orders from the Ministry of the Interior. According to Ercolani the order had been given by Minister Buffarini Guidi in a meeting with the prefects held in Florence. While this meeting did in fact take place, and it is likely that intended measures were outlined or announced, they were likely not yet definitive orders. The Grosseto measures emerged at the grassroots or peripheral level, from the prefect's interpretation, which anticipated future developments that appeared almost certain. This proves that it was possible for initiatives to move from the sidelines toward the center thanks to the zeal and enterprise of a single official (a phenomenon frequently identified in the Nazi system by the historiography of the Holocaust). On November 18, a German report expressed satisfaction with Ercolani's order for the internment of the Jews, praising the prefects of both Grosseto and Pisa as "energetic and dynamic" and for their "lively desire for loyal collaboration."[9] When asked for an explanation by the ministry, Ercolani replied: "Since detailed orders from the Directorate General [of Public Security] were awaited in vain, in order to fulfill the order, I believed setting up the camp was urgent and could not be delayed, entrusting its management to Gaetano Rizziello, Public Security officer of the Grosseto Police, who was recommended to me by the police chief as being highly capable and suitable for the post."[10]

The safety measures the prefect intended to employ around the camp required the involvement of members of the MVSN and *carabinieri*. The command of the 92nd Legion of the MVSN was ordered to "send 20 soldiers to the location with one officer equipped with at least two machine guns and two automatic rifles and an appropriate number of hand grenades per soldier. This unit, spread out along the wire fence, will be responsible for guarding the camp day and night [. . .]. The *carabinieri* force will maintain a permanent patrol unit outside the fences to ensure that no one, except authorized persons, approaches the camp and to provide the army with support for potential prison breaks."[11] The camp was to hold about sixty prisoners, including women, the elderly, and children, most of whom had turned themselves in following the prefect's internment orders. Post-Liberation documentation—contained in historian Luciana Rocchi's account—shows that the Roccatederighi camp was set up in the summer seminary of the Diocese of Grosseto. After the war, the bishop of Grosseto contacted the Ministry of the Interior to request the settlement of the outstanding rent. According to the contract signed by the bishop, "despite the need to reopen the seminary" the lease was granted "in response to a request arising from the emergencies of war" and "as proof of a special tribute to the new Government" of the RSI.[12] It is undeniable, therefore, that this lease was meant as an act of support—indeed, tribute—by the clergy.

By February 1944, as the fighting drew nearer, Prefect Ercolani was in a hurry to dismantle his camp, writing to the chief of police: "Please tell me where these [Jews] should be sent." Two buses belonging to a transport firm based in the town of Pitigliano and driven by civilians took the internees to the transit camp of Fossoli. According to one account, one of the bus drivers tried to contact the anti-Fascist partisans so that they might free the prisoners. But a rescue operation was never mobilized, and the bus reached its destination: the concentration and transit camp at Fossoli di Carpi, which had recently been taken over by the Germans.[13]

In Siena, as in Florence, the arrests of Jews began on November 5 and 6 and were under German direction by Theo Dannecker. He had been in charge of the group of men responsible for the Roman roundup of October 16, 1943, and had since moved north. However, local documentation shows that Italian Fascists also participated in these actions: "On the 5th of this month, the Jewess Lina Forti, daughter of Donato, was arrested by members of the MVSN and transferred to another location." In other cases, there is evidence of surveillance and searches. "The Jew Arturo Cabibbe, son of Cesare and Rosa Sadun, born in Florence on June 2, 1881, pharmaceutical representative, left for an unknown destination at the beginning of this month. Height 1.65 meters, heavy build, bald, sparse beard, decently dressed," wrote a Public Security marshal to the police chief of Siena on November 15, 1943.[14] A memorandum drafted after the war by a captain of the MVSN in defense of, and addressed to, the former prefect of Siena, Giorgio Alberto Chiurco, who was imprisoned at the time, attempted to play down the responsibilities of the Italians. Many Jews were not found in their homes: "I believe, in fact, that it was you who alerted them," wrote the captain, attempting to defend the prefect. "I am not sure how many were freed but I believe that it was the majority of those arrested. [...] [Some of them] recognized that we acted as humanely and honestly as possible." The captain recalled that during the operations he had met a soldier who admitted to him that "he did not really enjoy participating in that matter." At the same time, one of the families arrested by the MVSN recalled that another soldier had proudly proclaimed the actions underway, saying, "There are only two paths to take: one of honor, and one of dishonor. I have chosen that of honor."[15] While those responsible for the arrests all belonged to ideologically motivated paramilitary bodies, their attitudes toward their work could differ.

Also on November 5 and 6, 1943, this time in Montecatini, twenty-one Jews were arrested by Italians under German supervision. In fact, according to historian Valeria Galimi's reconstruction, the arrests were carried out by a "squad of at least six to eight fascists, together with Public Security agents who pursued the seizure under the command of two German officers."[16] Here, too, the presence of local Fascists had permitted or facilitated the house-to-house search. When questioned after the war, a vice-brigadier who had participated in the arrests justified his actions: "The presence of the Germans and armed fascists made it impossible for me to refuse. Subsequently, disgusted by what had happened, I managed—so as to avoid participating in similar matters—to leave the Public Security Office to work as an agent in the office of the Inspector General of Public Security, which did not involve any public security duties." (It was therefore possible to refuse specific assignments, apparently without consequences.)[17]

In Tuscany, as elsewhere in Italy, the order to arrest and intern Jews was followed by a steady stream of informing and arrests in the countless small towns and villages to which many Jews had fled, for example, in the areas around Pisa, Pistoia, and Livorno. One woman whose family, the Pipernos, had fled from Livorno to Staffoli, a hamlet near Santa Croce sull'Arno (Pisa), described how "after discovering that we were Jews, the owner of the house reported us to the local *carabinieri*. On the evening of December 23, 1944, the Fascists came to our house and took away my husband and my father-in-law." An officer from the Santa Croce *carabinieri* stood out in particular for the satisfaction and sense of bravado he seemed to display in carrying out his duties. Every time he took a Jew to the local prison he would address the other Jewish prisoners, saying, "There you go, I've brought you another one."[18] According to the testimony of the sole survivor of yet another roundup, on January 25, 1944, at Borgo a Buggiano (Pistoia), despite the protests of the priest who hosted them, local Fascists arrested eighteen Jews hidden in the rectory who had been reported by a "fascist from Livorno."[19] At Gabbro (Livorno), on December 20, 1943, a family of Greek origin from Livorno was arrested. "Our arrest can be ascribed to the marshal [of the *carabinieri*] from Gabbro who was also a member of a Fascist squad," explained the eighteen-year-old son of the family who was captured. "He arrested us all under his own initiative and handed us over to the Germans, possibly as a way of ingratiating himself to them."[20] At Ardenza, another small town near Livorno, in April 1944, Frida Misul was arrested together with her cousin after naïvely asking for help from an eminent lady in the Livornese Republican Fascist Party, who had advised her to ask the police for permission to enter the city. After being arrested, Frida beseeched the lady to help her. The lady's comment was: "I cannot do anything for Frida, because I do not want to risk my position, given that we are carrying out a campaign against the Jews who are ruining the world and are thus undesirable. Therefore I cannot obtain her release."[21] Frida Misul, who was deported to Auschwitz, would survive. She was liberated at Theresienstadt where she had been transferred and returned to tell her story.

Four

THE SEIZURE OF JEWISH PROPERTY

Starting with the enforcement of racial laws in the fall of 1938, the persecution of Jews by the Fascists resulted in both heavy limitations upon the economic activities of Italian Jews and the seizure of Jewish property. In the Republic of Salò, the plundering of Jewish property proceeded with renewed vigor, alongside individual persecution, toward a permanent solution. In order to act on their very existences, deciding their lives and their deaths, it was necessary to organize the impound and ultimately the confiscation of the victims' belongings—and to appropriate and relocate them.

The measures regarding "the racial question" announced in early November 1943 already contemplated confiscation of Jewish property. On November 24, 1943, the RSI Council of Ministers passed the first decree authorizing the seizure and confiscation of artistic, archaeological, historical, and bibliographical property owned by Jewish individuals or institutions. As previously described, even before the government launched its initiative, Prefect Ercolani of Grosseto had proactively introduced the generalized sequestration of Jewish property. He had prefaced his provisions by making explicit reference to the declarations of the Fascist party Congress of Verona, stating that the Jews were to be considered citizens belonging to an enemy nation of Italy. But, in the end, the arrest order issued on November 30, 1943, contained a provision for sequestration in anticipation of the confiscation of all Jewish assets and real estate.

Subsequently, on January 28, 1944, a new police order extended such seizures to all Jewish communities and provided for the dissolution of the same: "All Jewish communities shall be dissolved and their holdings seized." A number of prefects issued sequestration decrees, which took the atypical step of applying the status of physical persons to Jewish communities and institutions and called for these same communities "of the Jewish race" to be disbanded. This led to decrees such as that in Venice which stated "the Israelite Community of Venice belongs to the Jewish race and is therefore to be considered an enemy"; in Finale Emilia (near Modena), a similar decree read: "the Israelite Community of Finale Emilia belongs to the Jewish race."[1]

In the meantime, the legislative decree of January 4, 1944, had transformed seizures into confiscations and declared null and void any transfers of Jewish property to non-Jews that had taken place after November 30, 1943. Anyone who had contracted a debt with a Jew or who was in possession of Jewish property was required to inform the local prefect, who would confiscate such property on behalf of the state. The prefect would then hand it over for safekeeping, administration, and sale to the Ente di Gestione e Liquidazione Immobiliare (EGELI; Agency for the Management and Liquidation of [Jewish] Property), which had been set up in 1939 following the promulgation of the racial laws. The resulting revenue was to be donated by the state for the assistance, aid, and compensation for "war damage caused to the victims of enemy air raids." Lastly, in the final weeks of the RSI, the Fascist Council of Ministers approved a legislative decree on April 16, 1945, ratifying the dissolution of the Jewish communities already provided in a police order. Because of the upheavals of the political and military situation in the final days of the RSI, the decree was never enacted.

This persecutory framework contained measures specifying in detail how to allocate confiscated assets. Following the decree of January 4, 1944, EGELI was authorized to "sell at the best price" various types of property including "clothing, linen, blankets, or perishable goods often [confiscated] in small quantities or worth modest amounts." Or, "should sale prove difficult," it was to allocate them to the Ente Comunale di Assistenza (Municipal Assistance Agency [ECA]).[2] Other measures intertwined paradoxically with Jewish persecution. For example, the aforementioned decree of January 4, 1944, initially suspended pensions "assigned to persons of the Jewish race" but then resumed payments provided that these allowances were used for the "essential" purchase of food. Pensions were thereby limited to guaranteeing the very survival that these same authorities wished to render impossible or, following the agreements with the Germans, destroy. Many decades later, the Commission on the Spoliation of Jewish Assets—set up by the Italian state in 2001 and led by Italian Parliament member Tina Anselmi—issued its findings based on its reconstruction and analysis of the bureaucratic exchanges between the Ministry of Finance, the General Inspectorate of Race, and the prime minister's office. The commission remarked that in the correspondence between these agencies "there was no direct or indirect reference to the fact that the Jewish recipients of these pensions had already been arrested (by the RSI itself or by the Third Reich) and sent to Auschwitz or were busy going into hiding and changing their personal details on their documents."[3]

The Anselmi report identified the numerous irregularities and illegitimacies of the acts of spoliation—presuming that such acts could be considered legitimate, as they were in the legislative framework of the RSI. Many of these irregularities were the responsibility of the Ministry of the Interior itself. In June 1944, for example, Jewish goods and valuables that had been seized on the Italian-Swiss border were sent by the prefect of Como directly to the Directorate General of Public Security rather than to EGELI or a similar management agency as required under the new law. In another episode that took place during the first roundups of Jews in early December 1943, on the occasion of the seizure of thousands of pairs of socks and gloves belonging to a Jewish company ("worth approximately one million lire"), the proceeds were—in an unusual break with protocol—distributed between the Republican Fascist Party, the Ministry of the Interior, and the population. In fact, according to the Ministry of the Interior, the revenue was "largely allocated to the families of the Fallen in enemy raids."[4] Likewise—following an anonymous tip sent directly to Mussolini and rewarded with a payout of twenty-five thousand lire—the property confiscated from several

Jewish families from Mantua was transferred to the Ministry of the Interior, which sold it to "various officials of the Office of the Minister and of the Police." The remaining unsold items were replaced with old rags in their containers and according to the report filed by one of the victims after the Liberation, the confiscation order had assigned an essentially worthless value to the plundered goods, in part because their value had been deliberately underestimated but also because a considerable portion of the confiscated goods had not been officially listed. Many of the plundered assets remained in the possession of the organizations that had seized them. The Jewish Affairs Office of the Prefecture of Ferrara, for example, kept extremely slapdash accounts of confiscations, making it easier for various misappropriations to occur: in fact, there were no "entries for revenue from the sale of furniture." At that time, the prefect of this province had set up a bank account for the transfer of deposits confiscated from Jews and "made out in the name of the head of the Province of Ferrara [i.e., the prefect himself], who had the authority [. . .] to apply them to any operations that he might deem absolutely necessary and unavoidable."[5]

There were also cases in which single objects or valuables were stolen from the local offices of the Ministry of the Interior or Public Security. In Brescia, for example, the prefecture seized a piano from the Reinach family, as documented in a memorandum sent by the chief of police of Brescia to the prefect himself: "The Gors Bachman baby grand piano listed in the inventory was transported to the prefecture on January 18, [1944], in accordance with the verbal instructions given by this head of the prefect's office." In Como, the local police station "assigned" many meters of fabric seized from a Jewish firm but failed to record the recipients. Meanwhile the assets of "Doctor Cabibbe" were "sold to or gifted to or kept" by a certain "commissioner Masina." The former city commissioner of Como was ultimately held responsible for pinching goods worth twenty-five million lire. In Grosseto, the aforementioned prefect, Ercolani, had "arbitrarily skimmed" huge sums of money. While in Reggio Emilia, former police chief Pozzolini was the recipient of furniture belonging to the Melli household, which was "given for [his] use [. . .] and transported to his new headquarters."[6] The RSI Fascist State had therefore set up a vast persecutory system using legislative instruments that created complex administrative and bureaucratic mechanisms. At the same time, the representatives working for the state administration in various capacities and with varying responsibilities made provisions and carried out actions according to their own whims and in pursuit of personal profit or benefit.

The seizure of Jewish assets during the course of Italy's participation in the genocide took place not only through bureaucratic procedures but also in a series of episodes that amounted to true theft or robbery and were committed by single individuals or small groups. One such episode took place in Rome, in the fall of 1943. On the day immediately after the October 16 roundup, "just before seven o'clock," according to the morning report of the Roman police, "two uniformed fascists, accompanied by a young woman, entered the home of Mr. Piperno [Tranquillo Piperno, son of Samuele, resident of number 10, via Ferruccio], and left taking with them a large bundle whose contents are unknown." Another morning police report informs us that a few weeks later "at one o'clock, three individuals who identified themselves as members of Public Security entered the home of Giovanni Terracina, a Jew, on the second floor of 93 Piazza Monte d'Oro, and asked to speak to him. After roughing him up, they searched the place hoping to find gold bars. When their search proved fruitless, they demanded that Terracina hand over the sum of 250,000 lire. When Terracina complained that he did not have such a sum of money they reduced their demands to 70,000 lire [. . .]. Toward five o'clock, after eating a meal made up of food they found in the apartment, the three individuals left after informing Terracina that they would return the following day to collect the 20,000 lire still outstanding." (They had in the meantime been able to collect 50,000 lire from both Terracina and a displaced woman, probably not Jewish, who lived in the same apartment and provided the majority of the sum.)[7]

A section of the 2001 Anselmi report describes material damages suffered by the Jews from 1938 to 1945 and lists numerous episodes of spoliation that took place concurrently or after Jewish arrests by Italians. However, it only scratches the surface of the many episodes that were described in a series of postwar testimonies registered at the Center for Contemporary Jewish Documentation of Milan. In January 1949, for example, Pia Levi, a lawyer from Ravenna, reported that civil proceedings had been lodged against the city's police chief and prefect, who had threatened the building administrators and occupied the apartments belonging to Jews who had either fled or been arrested. According to a deposition given in 1946 by the president of the Jewish Community of Turin, not only did the infamous Fascist Fracchia line his pockets with the rewards paid by the SS for every arrested Jew, he also confiscated any valuables the victims had on their persons including "cash, jewelry, and watches." In his deposition we read that "Fracchia made truly significant profits from his activities. [. . .] confirmed indirectly by the furnishings in his home." The testimony given by another witness after the war describes what happened to a family from Ferrara: "At that time people were talking about searches being made in the homes of Jews [. . .]. One evening two members of the fascist militia turn up at my house. They say everything in the house is Jewish property, which entitles them to seize and search everything [. . .]. An anonymous tip informed them that the hallway, dining room, and two bedrooms as well as the studies on the ground floor are all full of furniture, linen, and silverware." Such anonymous tips abounded during the months of the arrests. "We have been informed that the silverware belonging to the Jew Giorgio Sonnino and worth a huge amount is hidden in the home of Engineer C. L.," stated one of these reports, specifying that "[it] has been placed inside a wall cavity" and that "more specific information [. . .] could be obtained by questioning the members of C. L.'s family as well as Lisetta, their former maid."

Adding insult to injury, in November 1949, EGELI demanded payment of the sum of 5,473 lire from a victim of confiscation for the "administration of tasks necessary at the time to confiscate assets at the victim's expense, per the measures adopted under the repealed racial laws. The total not including additional interest owed."[8]

Daily episodes of the abuse of power and violence following the confiscations or instances when the would-be plunderers were left empty-handed were all too frequent. Files on seizures, confiscations, and reappropriations piled up on the desks of bureaucrats, administrators, and ministers of the Social Republic. Often, they concerned Jews who had already been arrested, sent to extermination camps, or killed, whose property would now make other Italians rich. Several years after the war, the wheels of state bureaucracy continued to grind forward relentlessly, insisting that the victims, most of whom had yet to be compensated, pay the administrative costs borne by the public in subjecting them to those abuses.

Five

DECEMBER 1943

Arrests and Deportations from Venice

Following the November 30, 1943, order for the arrest of Italian Jews, the chief of police of Venice, Filippo Cordova, while still awaiting precise instructions, told the city's police and *carabinieri* to "caution" all Jews "not to leave their place of residence and to report at the nearest Public Security office or Carabinieri Command." His telegram also specified that "the most influential and dangerous Jews are to be placed under guard in their homes."[1] Stereotypical anti-Jewish propaganda had insinuated itself into the bureaucratic imagination, diffusing an exaggerated vision of the supposed influence and dangerous nature of the Jews who were still living in Venice, confined to their homes since the start of the German occupation in early September.

Finally the minister's instructions arrived: "All Jews, even those who have been exonerated, whatever their nationality, who are residents within the national territory, shall be interned in special concentration camps; their personal possessions and real estate shall be impounded and then confiscated in the interest of the Italian Social Republic, which will distribute it for the benefit of the homeless who were made so by enemy air raids." He concluded with the following order: "In the meantime the Jews shall be interned in provincial camps to await transfer to specially designed concentration camps."[2] With this order Italian authorities had officially and directly initiated the persecution of the Jews. We know that in many other cities arrests had been taking place for some weeks in that tragic fall of 1943. Only a few days later, following painstaking preparations in the wake of the ministerial order, Venice would launch its own police operation, using the lists of names that were drawn up after the racist census of 1938 and had been constantly updated. At 2:00 p.m., on December 5, 1943, the chief of police gave orders for the "immediate arrest of elements belonging to the Jewish race." This order, which was sent to the Public Security offices, Carabinieri command, and the 49th Legion of the MVSN, involved not only the police and military forces of the reborn Fascist State but also the armed wing of the party.

The arrests were carried out at night, under the cover of darkness, to conceal actions that could have been met with public disapproval and to take the designated victims by surprise while they slept or, in any case, in their homes. Police stations had lists of the addresses of the Jews in their respective neighborhoods and could send various units to the homes of the individual families whose whereabouts had been confirmed over the previous days. The agents would ring the bell and go up to the floor indicated in the documents, a door would open, and the head of the family and all the family members would be identified. How would the policemen, *carabinieri*, and Fascist squad members have spent that evening prior to the

arrests? After hastily eating a frugal meal at home, they
would have mumbled, "I'm on duty tonight too." "They
told us to get ready and meet up at the station this evening." "They've given an order to arrest the Jews." Why?
What've they done? "It's the war. They're foreigners and
enemies. They can't be trusted." "There's a war on. Everyone
has to pay. The Jews even more so because they're profi-
teers." Where are they taking them? "To a concentration
camp. And then we'll see." "To Germany and then the
Germans will deal with them." Silence. They put on their
uniforms, went out into the cold night, and went to the
station to receive their orders. Volunteers from the Fascist party accompanied the policemen to the houses and
patrolled the areas where the prisoners were being held.
"The aforementioned [Jews]," ordered the telegram, "will
be transported to the local prison of Santa Maria Maggiore, to the Giudecca Penitentiary, if female, and to the
juvenile center, if minors." The transfer took place in Venice partly on foot and partly by boat. Did anyone put
up resistance? Not that we know of, or at least no cases
of people resisting arrest were recorded. Certainly there
would have been requests for explanations, pleas, protests at being separated from other family members, un-
certainty about what the future held. What were they allowed to take with them? Only a few things. How long
will we be gone? No reply.

On the following evening, the prefect informed the
Ministry of the Interior about the successful outcome of
the operation: "On the night of the 6th of this month, in
Venice and the surrounding province, 163 pure-blooded
Jews were arrested, 114 of whom are women and 49 are
men." Their operations were already being carried out

in coordination with the Germans: "In accord with the local German command, Jews with an Aryan spouse or vice versa were not yet arrested but remain under guard. Awaiting further instructions." The operation lasted all night. By dawn most of the arrestees had been taken to the prison of Santa Maria Maggiore; others were at the Marco Foscarini boarding school, which was also being used as barracks by the Fascist National Republican Guard and to house evacuees and refugees; the minors were kept in various institutions. The following week, however, the prisoners would be transferred to the Casa di Ricovero Israelitica (Jewish Rest House), a convalescent home in the Ghetto Nuovo, which was used as a transit camp and was guarded by Public Security agents.

In the following days, three police agents went to each address where they had arrested either a single Jew or Jewish family and expropriated their homes. First they drew up detailed lists of the property's contents— although single objects may have been left off the lists and removed—and then sealed the house. On December 28, the Venice police chief informed the police stations and Carabinieri command of the transfer of the Jews to the Fossoli di Carpi transit camp, the stopover before deportation to Poland: "The Ministry of the Interior has given orders for all Jews arrested in this Province to be transferred to the Carpi concentration camp. The Jews are to take with them their bedding, mattresses, sheets, blankets, pillowcases, and pillows."[3] No time was lost in arranging the transfer: on December 31, the Public Security commissioner of the Venetian Railways communicated the departure of ninety-three Jews "escorted by *carabinieri*"; those over seventy years of age and Jewish children from mixed marriages were initially spared. "They occupied two third-class carriages made available by the Italian Railways," specified the telegram, "while their personal effects, totaling about 1,500 kilos, were transported in a freight car attached to their convoy." A statement given after the war describes how the Jews were transferred from the convalescent home in the Venetian Jewish quarter.[4]

Yet again everything took place at night. A *carabiniere* asked the non-Jewish handyman employed by the hospice turned transit camp to procure a large boat. "They told me to hire a large boat," wrote the man in a report several years later, "and to take the Jews interned in the hospice by night to the rail station, traveling via the back canals." The handyman countered that they could use the public ferry boats—either out of concern for the comfort of the passengers or to complicate matters and attempt some resistance. "There are no ferry boats," replied the *carabiniere*, annoyed. He did not wish to use public transport or call upon others for the transfer arrangements because this would inevitably have led to further contacts, authorizations, and red tape. In the end they decided to use a specially requisitioned ferry boat that would leave from a nearby stop. But to get there the group of Jewish prisoners, accompanied by an armed escort, first had to walk in procession through the *calli*, or narrow alleys leading from the Ghetto Nuovo to the San Marcuola landing. Here they boarded the boat that glided a few hundred meters along the Grand Canal to the nearby railway station. Did anyone see them and ask what was happening? And if so, what were their reactions? Some of these questions are answered by the handyman. "I watched the boat at the San Marcuola landing, guarded by police agents and *carabinieri*, and went to wait for those unfortunate souls at the nearby Ponte dei Scalzi (the bridge by the railway station), but, because there were so many curious onlookers, some muttering disapproving comments under their breath for fear of spies, the ferry boat continued past the passenger landing to a pier used to unload building materials for the station, which was under construction." After getting off at the railway station, "the passengers took their places, confident of a swift return, in two third-class carriages." His account continues, "In the meantime, I placed their sealed luggage in two freight cars, and although the doors were locked and in spite of the usual *carabiniere* who forbade me to, I managed to get the travel papers to Dottor Muggia, promising that I would pick them up upon their return and bidding them farewell." So they hoped to return? They certainly wanted to hope, or were made to hope.

The Venetian roundup was one of the largest carried out by the Italians in December 1943. The events of Venice in those days are described in a letter written by one of the arrestees. It is unusual in that it is one of the few documents that give us a firsthand account of the arrests from a victim. It is not a black-and-white depiction of events—as we might tend to assume—but a letter containing all the gray shades of reality. It is a letter from a father, written shortly before his transfer to the Fossoli camp, to his son who had escaped arrest.[5]

Since early December, there had been rumors in Venice that a roundup and subsequent deportation were imminent. Some had said that the Fascists were "waiting for trucks to come and pick us up." But the letter's author had not "taken those words at face value." "How often had they attempted to scare us—sometimes successfully—just with the aim of fraying our nerves?" On the night of December 5, the operation was finally launched. The letter is by someone unfamiliar with writing who uses rather colloquial language to express himself: "At a quarter to three we were woken by a ring at the door. First we thought it was one of the usual rascals, but at the second ring we got up and asked who was there. The response: 'It's the police.'" Everything proceeded in a relatively orderly manner. "Remember dear Pino that I told you that things [. . .] would happen, but in a lawful manner[?]" The letter writer continues with his reconstruction, confirming his own expectations: "In fact, no brutish faces, just the police chief, four local policemen in plainclothes, and two *carabinieri*." "After hearing that we four would be required to report at the station, I asked the police chief if we could take our luggage with us and some money for our travel expenses." "In the meantime," he recalls, "he asked me who owned the house, and who lived on the first and second floors." There was even time to prepare coffee. "Given that he [the police chief] had asked to see all the tenants, I asked for permission to put the coffee on."

They were then taken to the police station—on foot and without incident ("We were convinced by now that we would have to leave") or rough treatment. "The police commissioner calmly and politely handed us over to the plainclothes officers, who kindly carried our bags to the San Marco police station." Here they found "eight men, all much older than me, and five very elderly women."

And again they could still enjoy some moments of freedom: "They allowed us to go to the bar for a coffee, obviously accompanying us, but they were all nothing if not polite." The hours passed, and orders gradually arrived all morning, specifying the destinations of the arrestees: "We hear a phone call being received in the police chief's office and they tell us: men to [the prison of] Santa Maria Maggiore, women to Giudecca [the island where the women's prison was located] and children to the reform schools." Late that same morning "a boat arrived for the detainees [...] and [we were] off to Santa Maria Maggiore." And it was here that the family experienced their most painful moment when their little daughter Nedda was taken away, although the prison director had initially agreed to let her stay with her parents, so long as he did not receive a countercommand from the police headquarters. "That is, my dear Pino, when we experienced our worst moment. A policeman took Nedda away from us, gently but away nonetheless, and the scream she let out, I can assure you dear Pino [...] I will always feel that scream here in my heart and not knowing where they had taken her weighed so heavily upon me."

Once in the prison they were questioned separately, and lists were drawn up of their personal items and money ("which were given back to us afterward"). "So nine in a cell and then came that terrible night, the real prison experience, something I'll tell you about if God sees fit to reunite us one day." In the following days the prisoners received comfort and assistance from the prison chaplain and "Monsignor Urbani from the Patriarchate [of Venice]." Eight days later they were released—or, more precisely, transferred to a new place of internment: the Casa di Ricovero Israelitica, the convalescent home in Venice's Jewish quarter. Yet again their forced transfer took place at night: "Finally the order of release to take us, by night of course, because God forbid that someone sees us." And the letter adds, "As if the public voicing of disapproval and true human fraternity had not been clearly expressed by the whole of Catholic Venice." (The writer is probably referring to the visits and messages received from the Venetian clergy.) "To take us ... here to the convalescent home where there were about 140 of us." (He is probably excluding those over seventy years old.)

Nedda was finally reunited with her parents. The letter continues by describing the living conditions in the convalescent home: "We all did just fine there [...] also with daily visits from everyone, too many at times." There were even daily prayers and Sabbath prayers. They began to settle into daily life there. A few weeks later, however, they were transferred to the Fossoli camp, a destination still unknown to most of the prisoners: "This morning a brigadier came from the police headquarters and told us to be ready by the 30th of the month because they had received orders to send us to the concentration camp. Where to we do not know, they just told us to get ready and to take our mattresses, bedding, and food with us. Dear Pino, our ordeal has yet to end and God only knows if I'll be able to let you know our whereabouts or even if we'll ever see each other again. I trust in God and hope you do too, and let's hope that with his help we will."

On December 31, 1943, therefore, ninety-three Jews left Venice for Fossoli di Carpi. On January 18, 1944, they would be followed by a group of very young minors whose "previous conditions had prevented them from traveling." Had they been sick? Had they been in the custody of someone who was trying to save them? We do not know. The provincial police commissioner gave instructions for these children to be reunited with their parents,[6] which meant sending them to the same lethal fate. Were the police forces aware of this fate? If so, to what extent, and did they know the details? Was it possible not to contemplate this fate, or not to suspect it whatever their destination may have been? Attached to the order sent by the provincial police commissioner to the Fossoli camp director was a list of the children who were to be accompanied on the train by "agents from this office": "Mario Levi, son of Beniamino, aged 4; Lino Levi, son of Beniamino, aged 6; Sergio Todesco, son of Eugenio, aged 4; Mara Nacamulli, daughter of Eugenio, aged 3."[7] How did the children act and how were they looked after on the journey? Did any of the agents consider refusing to participate or attempt to change their route or find another destination for the young prisoners? What would have been the consequences had they done so? About one month later, on February 22, 1944, these same minors, recently reunited with their parents, were in the convoy that left Fossoli for Auschwitz. Among them was one of the few prisoners who would manage to find his way back after the war: Primo Levi. He and the other 649 prisoners, all crammed into the twelve freight cars, would make the four-day journey to the Polish camp.[8]

Over the following weeks and months, the Venetian police headquarters continued to confiscate and inventory

Jewish property; to hunt down Jews who had eluded the December roundup; and to keep watch over the elderly aged over seventy, the sick, Jews married to Aryans, and children of "mixed" marriages between Jews and "Aryans." Police documents reveal the particular dedication with which police stations surveilled both elderly and pregnant women. Jews hospitalized at the Venice Ospedale Civile (Civil Hospital) were placed under armed guard, as were the elderly who had been left behind in the Casa di Ricovero and who were required to conscientiously report every movement—mostly hospital visits—beforehand. This control would help the German SS make their arrests in Venice in the summer of 1944. Their operations, which extended to the Ospedale Civile and the asylum for the mentally ill on the island of San Servolo, were conducted under the command of Captain Franz Stangl, the former commandant of the camps of Sobibor and Treblinka. The arrests were carried out with the assistance, on the ground, of Mauro Grini, a Jewish collaborationist from Trieste, whom I will come back to, and of the Public Security office of the Ospedale Civile, which supplied organizational support under the direction of "Marshal Casella [. . .] who accompanied Stangl to the Custody Room" where a number of Jews had found shelter, according to the reconstruction offered in a letter written after the war by a Jewish patient who had managed to survive.[9]

The documentation of the Venetian police contains a number of details with regard to some of the elderly and "mixed-blood" Jews under careful surveillance. On December 27, 1943, following the incarceration, transfer to the Casa di Ricovero, and then release on grounds of age of Elena Fano, a Jewish woman over seventy years old, the police headquarters instructed the San Marco police station to "trace and place under surveillance the Jewess [. . .] residing in San Marco 2055 with her siblings." The lady in question and her brothers, who were also elderly, were finally deported by the Germans in the summer of 1944 and killed upon their arrival at Auschwitz.[10] On May 3, 1944, the Cannaregio police station informed police headquarters that seventy-seven-year-old Bice Castelnuovo, who was of "the Jewish race and religion," continued to live alone in her home. Signora Castelnuovo was "warned not to leave the city," and orders were given to place her "under suitable surveillance":[11] in the end, she was spared from deportation. On March 31, 1944, a police officer informed police headquarters that a Jewish woman married to a Catholic "Aryan" was in the hospital "waiting to give birth." Fifteen days later, the police headquarters hurriedly sought to learn whether this evidently "dangerous" subject had returned to her home: they also asked that the members of her family be specified and gave orders for the woman to be placed under "suitable surveillance."[12]

As we have seen, the police continued to confiscate Jewish property, often with the collaboration of ordinary citizens who reported and informed on their neighbors and acquaintances. The prefect of Venice, for example, informed the police chief that Mr. F. C., who was living in the commandeered apartment of Mrs. Amalia Cesana, had submitted the list of furnishings, pointing out, however, that some items were missing, including "mattresses, blankets, linen, ornaments, clothing, and table- and kitchenware." The gentleman concerned was "under the belief" and keen to suggest that said objects "had been concealed" in the homes of the "Aryan" relatives of Mrs. Cesana.[13] Other reports concerned elderly Jews still living in their homes on the Venetian mainland, such as the Erreras, who remained in their villa at Mirano. In this particular case the arrest and most of the plundering were carried out by the Germans, while the Italians functioned as drivers, movers, or interpreters. The incident is documented in detail in a report by the GNR.[14] After forcing his way into the Erreras' home, a German officer interrogated the elderly couple with the help of his Italian interpreter, recognized them as Jews, and gave orders for them to be arrested and taken to Venice. "He then proceeded to seize all the assets in the house and ordered the couple to hand over any valuables (passbooks, cash, etc.). He took the gold bracelet and pearl necklace that the old lady was wearing, carried out a body search, and then arrested the aforementioned, who were driven to Venice by Germans and then taken to the Santa Maria Maggiore prison." The National Guard soldier here paused in his report to give the ages of the couple: "Paolo Errera is eighty-two years of age and his wife is over seventy." Despite the lengthy description of their interrogation, pat down, and arrest, he concluded laconically with the words: "No violence was used."[15]

In the end, the Italians also got their hands on the Erreras' belongings to the extent that the local police headquarters ordered a so-called "protective sequestration" of the remaining property.[16] In the summer of 1944, the local police discovered various pieces of the Erreras' silver in the home of a Miranese man who claimed that "he was temporarily using the property belonging to the Jew

Paolo Errera, which was in his home with the permission of Marshal Vincenzo Nocera, former Commandant of the National Guard contingent."[17] The protective sequestration measures, therefore, were effective only to a certain point. After the Liberation, during the attempt to uncover the whereabouts of the Erreras' assets, Amedeo Vincenti, a former major of the GNR, stated—by way of example—that he had "per regulation accepted delivery of" eleven linen sheets and seven pillowcases at the villa on behalf of the former prefect, Piero Cosmin, "for use in the personal residence of the prefect, reserved for him by the Venetian police." Following an order given by the same prefect, various pieces of furniture were taken to "furnish the official quarters of the chief of police."[18] During his interrogation the confiscator of the bed linen remarked that "there were only three sheets belonging to the State in the prefect's entire apartment. Hence," he concluded, "it was necessary to take stuff belonging to Jews."[19]

In the case of Villa Fano on the Venetian island of Lido, the sequestration of the building and its contents was carried out by Fascists and in the end the Germans would also benefit. Jewish homes were frequently commandeered after their owners were arrested or if their whereabouts were considered untraceable after they fled. This was the case of the Lido villa of entrepreneur Vittorio Fano, who fled to Switzerland with his family in 1943, returned to Venice immediately after the war, and became president of the reestablished Jewish Community of Venice. When Fano filed a report on a series of thefts, the Office for the Restitution of Jewish Property (Ufficio Recupero Beni Ebraici) of the Venice police headquarters questioned those involved, thus revealing what had actually happened to Fano's home and to some of his assets during the period of the Republic of Salò and the German occupation of Venice.[20]

Initially, Antonio Tomasella, an acquaintance of the Fano family, had agreed with the owners to move into the house "to look after the contents during their temporary absence." In the fall of 1943, however, "through the Lido branch of the Fascist party," two families who had moved to Venice to work for the Salò administration took up residence at the house. According to Tomasella, the new arrivals "took over the whole villa, trying to force me and my mother to move out." He was in effect evicted from the house and his place was taken by the secretary of the local Fascist party: "By refusing to give way and making complaints to the local Fascist party I managed to continue living in the villa until one day, when I was out of town for family reasons, a certain Guerrieri, the local head of the Fascist party, forced my mother to leave the house and moved into the newly vacated rooms with his family."[21] When questioned, Guerrieri, who had been incarcerated after the Liberation for his involvement with the Fascist Party during the Republic of Salò, claimed that in January 1944, "under the terms of the requisition order by the former Republican Prefecture of Venice," he had managed to "occupy part of the villa owned by the Israelite Vittorio Fano," after having submitted a request to the prefect motivated by "the lack of space in the dwelling where he currently resided."[22] But the new families who had been assigned Fano's villa did not merely occupy the building: "On several occasions I [Tomasella] noticed that [. . .] the members of the Magnolfi family used the contents of the villa as if they were their own, and they often organized shipments of packing cases, trunks, and other large packages":[23] these items, along with various pieces of furniture, were included in the report filed by Fano after the Liberation. The Lido Fascist Party secretary was also called upon to explain what had occurred: in addition to the objects and household linen that he had assigned to various "indigent families from Lido or removed from the occupied properties," he was asked to explain why an empty trunk and other items belonging to the Fano family had been found in his home.[24] It seems, moreover, that the new occupants of the Villa Fano were not content with occupying the house and stealing some of its contents: in fact, according to Tomasella, Fabiano Magnolfi—described in Fano's report as a "member of a fascist squad [*squadrista*], formerly employed by the Ministry of Agriculture and Forestry of the former Social Republic"—"asked me on numerous occasions for information on the whereabouts of the villa's owners in order to arrest them." He went on to explain that "he [Magnolfi] kept the photographs of the members of the Fano family in his pocket in the hope of possibly identifying them."[25] Thus we have an ordinary citizen, an average Italian employed by the Salò administration (albeit a *squadrista* according to a contemporary report), preparing to track down, or at the very least report on, the family of Jews whose house he was occupying. Arrest, deportation, and flight were followed by sequestration, confiscation, occupation, and theft. Sometimes even after their homes had been occupied, the hunt for Jews continued.

Six

Hunting Down Jews in Florence

The first Florentine roundup took place at dawn on November 6, 1943. It was carried out by the same German military forces responsible for the Roman roundup of October 16 who had since moved northward. However, according to an eyewitness report recounted after the Liberation, the attack on the synagogue—during the course of which the temple was surrounded and invaded, rounds of shots were fired, and sacred objects and sections of the interior were destroyed—saw the involvement of "Italian Fascists in plainclothes." According to this same account, "In the following days, the Republican fascists stripped the offices and the school of all furnishings. The archive, the books from the temple and the office, firewood, and *taledoth* [ritual shawls] were all sold and mostly bought as old junk by a coal merchant."[1] The attacks spread throughout the city, leading to the arrest of many of the foreign Jews sheltering with Jewish assistance organizations and—with lists of names in hand—reaching the homes of individual Florentine Jews. The roundup probably led to more than a hundred arrests, and some Fascists participated even at this stage, acting as guides for the Germans as they made their way through the city.

Among those arrested were Professor Augusto Gallico, along with his wife and two children (one aged ten), captured "by German soldiers with trucks driven by Fascists."[2]

A raid carried out a few weeks later saw the involvement, along with the Germans, of one of the most vicious actors of Florentine Republican Fascism: the Carità gang. On the night between November 16 and 17, the infamous gang took part in the raid on the Franciscan convent in the Piazza del Carmine where numerous Jewish women and their children had taken refuge. They were held prisoner in the convent for four days before being transferred to Verona by truck—the Fossoli camp was not yet operational—and deported from there to Auschwitz. The raid was carried out by about thirty soldiers—both German and Italian—and one of the survivors described how the Fascists guarding the prisoners subjected the women to sexual molestation and extortion.[3]

The deportation of the Florentine Jews and the spoliation of their property could not have taken place without the assistance of three Italian entities playing a crucial political and organizational role. They were the aforementioned Carità gang, the Office of Jewish Affairs, and the local police headquarters, all three of which received the full support of the city's Fascist prefecture. The notorious brutality of the gang led by Major Mario Carità, or, as it was officially known, the Special Services Branch of the 92nd Legion of the MVSN, has led to the widespread belief that it acted independently. However, this group too was part of the Fascist military body of the RSI and therefore operated in close coordination with both the prefecture and the Office of Jewish Affairs. During the first months of the group's activity, Carità drew up a political orientation document, sending it to Mussolini himself in December 1943. In it, he called for a return to Fascism's original *squadrismo* (i.e., the paramilitary phase of the origins) and for a "totalitarian renewal" in order to combat the enemies of the RSI, whom he described as "infected ganglia to be extirpated."[4] In addition to participating in raids in the local area, the Carità gang also carried out its activities in a number of Florentine villas, which they used as their headquarters, as detention centers, and to carry out torture sessions. Before Carità and his men installed themselves in the infamous Villa Triste on Via Bolognese, sharing the building with the Germans, they requisitioned the homes of two Jewish families—the Forti and Loria families—who had managed to flee in time.

According to the scrupulous reconstruction of historian Marta Baiardi, while antisemitic persecution "undoubtedly took second place to the anti-partisan activities [of the Carità gang], it was neither sporadic nor negligible" and was "mainly motivated by ends linked to profit and extortion, and was even carried out autonomously by individual unit members." In the absence of statements explicitly referring to actions by the Carità gang that were ideologically motivated by antisemitism, Baiardi believes that Carità and his henchmen considered the Jews "prey at their mercy, inoffensive because they were harmless and completely defenseless, but insignificant."[5] Still, typical of the gang's antisemitic practices was their frequent extortion of Jewish property by the Carità gang in exchange for a guarantee of protection or safety, before reneging on such promises (Lieutenant Ferdinando Manzella, a former Fascist secret police agent with a long criminal record, excelled in this).[6]

While Carità and his supporters cannot, strictly speaking, be numbered among ideologically motivated executioners, they pursued Jewish victims because of the overarching genocidal situation, its norms (or lack thereof), and its hierarchies. The presumed insignificance of their victims was also the result of their degradation and dehumanization imposed by the rationale of persecution. Sometimes Carità's Jewish quarry was caught up in his net in a sudden, almost casual manner. According to a report produced by the Florentine police headquarters after the liberation of the city, the major was in the habit of walking around "accompanied by four or six henchmen" who were armed and "making quick, desultory appearances in various public places in the city, where he [Carità] would occasionally arrest the odd Israelite pointed out to him by his hangers-on and informants."[7]

On December 3, 1943 (shortly after the order for the arrest of the Jews issued by the RSI), Carità and his unit, who were in the area of Greve in Chianti where they had probably aborted a failed anti-partisan operation, decided to raid the villa belonging to Goffredo Passigli, a Jewish industrialist from Florence who had been a Fascist during Mussolini's regime. They arrested both him and his two sons aged twenty and thirty, after having surrounded the property. Some believe that the family was betrayed by the manager—and after the 1938 antisemitic laws, the legal representative—of the Passigli stocking factory, although the woman was cleared of all charges after the war. When interrogated after the Liberation, the Fascists from Greve stated that Carità had originally planned to capture partisans, but the Passigli family's arrest was nevertheless "a big catch." According to another contemporary reconstruction, Carità had expressed great satisfaction at having tracked down Passigli, exclaiming "repeatedly that the day had not been in vain and that it was an even greater coup to have captured Passigli than the partisans."[8] While the possibility of making a profit would certainly have played a role, the chronological correlation with the order for the arrest of all Italian Jews tells us that, in bureaucratic terms, the hunt for Jews had only just been added to the daily agenda by the Italian authorities. Passigli and his sons, the casual collateral victims of an anti-partisan raid, would end up dying at Auschwitz.

The true base of Florence's anti-Jewish persecutions was the Office of Jewish Affairs, set up by the prefecture in the heart of the city on Via Cavour, in offices commandeered from the Jewish lawyer Errera. The Office of Jewish Affairs was headed by Giovanni Martelloni, an intransigent Fascist with a long criminal record who was a personal friend of the prefect Manganiello. The office was established during the period of the Social Republic as the political and organizational branch of the local Center for the Study of the Jewish Problem, which was part of a network of centers in various Italian cities created by the Ministry of Popular Culture in the 1940s. Martelloni began his career there in 1942, producing antisemitic propaganda alongside the center's other clerks, who would also become active persecutors working for the new office. During the Salò period, the police and militia activities targeting Jews were flanked by Martelloni's propaganda work, which included the production of purportedly "historic" material on the Jews in Florence. His articles appeared in the city's Fascist press, and in April 1944, this diligent antisemitic functionary wrote an introduction and commentary for a collected volume of anti-Jewish laws. The Office of Jewish Affairs sought to centralize, or at least lay claim to, anti-Jewish activities in Florence, and in March 1944 it succeeded in obtaining the authority to issue and sign provisions and decrees for the confiscation of Jewish property. A postwar investigation discovered that Martelloni and his cohort had "made a profit from the confiscated property of Jews that had come into the possession of the Office."[9] Among the center's most active employees was Pier Luigi Brilli, who not only organized the confiscation of the bauble and needlework business owned by Leone Camerino, who had since been deported, but also took charge of its "socialization," to use the new RSI watchword. This included redistributing among the employees the salaries of three Jewish workers who had concealed themselves to avoid arrest. According to Baiardi, Brilli exemplifies the mentality of the Salò political class, which "consisted of an (indigestible) mixture of unrealistic ideologies, both petty and serious graft, and obtuse indifference with regard to the related human costs."[10]

Martelloni's office bestowed Florence with a key national role in the persecution of Jews by the Italian forces owing to its characteristic "blend of intense rapaciousness and virulent antisemitism." Martelloni and his team were tragically effective in carrying out and supervising every stage of the anti-Jewish persecution developed by the RSI, including the "arrest, internment, spoliation, and management of the property [of the Jews]."[11] This was possible thanks to data—personal information in particular—inherited from the Center for the Study of the Jewish Problem and to coordination with the aforementioned police bodies in addition to many other agencies such as the Revenue Bureau (Intendenza di Finanza), the Fine Arts Superintendence, local town authorities of the surrounding area, police headquarters, police stations, *carabinieri*, and German commands. The mocking indifference and pitilessness distinguishing the procedures carried out by Martelloni's staff are exemplified by what occurred after the arrest of the elderly Jewish proprietors of the Emporio Duilio department store in Florence. According to the couple's son, one day, the sequestrator of the company, Antonio Marinetto, a Republican Fascist with a criminal record, invited all the store staff to "a splendid lunch to celebrate the business having achieved total independence" (i.e., from its Jewish owners).[12] Alongside the systematic sequestrations, others recalled with terror the apparently random violence that could erupt during Martelloni's strolls around the city, during which he would, from time to time, produce the photographs of wanted Jews from his coat pocket.[13]

Research has shown that, unlike in the rest of Italy, in Florence and the surrounding province, the police and *carabinieri* played a secondary role in the persecution of Jews in comparison to the Office of Jewish Affairs, the Fascist militia (GNR), and the Carità gang. However, the arrest system, which worked efficiently and to the detriment of entire families, was more than just a bureaucratic process; it was rooted in a "low-intensity" antisemitism "made up of an acquiescence to the legitimate authority, a dulling of consciences, and a shared non-egalitarian vision of society," intensified by the recent years of anti-Jewish propaganda and a substrate of Catholic anti-Judaism.[14]

Occasionally, in smaller towns and villages, administrative staff would act as either primary or auxiliary bureaucratic executors of persecutory provisions. For example, two employees of the Municipality of Impruneta, a small town near Florence, were involved in the arrest of the Spizzichino-Calò family. The municipal guard acted as the driver of the vehicle transporting them to the police station, while the secretary of the Municipal Council assisted the *carabinieri* in drawing up the inventory of the family's household property. On March 13, 1944, at Cascio di Reggello, in the Valdarno area, yet another Calò family was subjected to arrest, this time carried out, even if only in a bureaucratic sense, by a local *carabinieri* marshal, who thus reconstructed the events in a postwar trial: "I tried to warn the Calò family so that they could save themselves. Some of them left the town immediately, while others, such as the daughter-in-law [Carolina Lombroso] with her children, did not wish to go, and so, in spite of my own wishes, I had no choice but to carry out the warrant for their arrest. I repeat that the order was issued by police headquarters."[15] So the bureaucratic persecutor had attempted to mitigate—or even prevent—the effects of his own actions (or at least so he claimed), while at the same time justifying his deeds by evoking the impossibility, whether real or presumed, of failing to carry out his orders.

The family that he arrested at Cascio di Reggello—Carolina, Elena (aged seven), Renzo (aged five), and Albertino (aged two)—were the wife and children of Eugenio Calò, who would later be awarded the Gold Medal for Military Valor in the Resistance. Carolina may have given birth to their fourth child during their grueling seven-day journey to Auschwitz.[16] Some members of the family had therefore escaped—apparently after being warned by the *carabinieri* marshal beforehand—while others—including children between the ages of two and seven (and probably also a newborn)—were thus condemned to death thanks to the effective contribution of the Italian executioners—the harbingers of the genocide of the Jews on the banks of the river Arno.

Seven

AT THE BORDER

Jews on the Run

The situation facing the Jews fleeing the provinces of central Italy and, above all, northern Italy to seek refuge in Switzerland, a neutral country seen as a land of safety, was dramatic and often ended in tragedy. Although many found shelter beyond the border, many more were sent back or arrested before reaching it. Among those who reached it and subsequently were actually registered at the border, 6,000 were admitted, while almost 8,700 were turned away. Arrests were carried out not only by the Germans controlling the border areas but also by the Italian border patrol, police, the Guardia di Finanza (a military branch of police responsible for the enforcement of customs, excise, and tax), and the GNR units (whose ranks included the *carabinieri*). One hundred twenty-two of the 185 people who ended up in Italian custody in the prison of Miogni, near Varese, were arrested along the border—and over half of that number were arrested by Italian forces. Others, including 28 people arrested in Varese, or who hailed from the provinces bordering Como and Sondrio, were incarcerated in the prison of Como or sent directly to San Vittore prison in Milan.[1] The Germans began their hunt for Jews in late October 1943, while the Italians arrested their first Jew on October 11. That day the Guardia di Finanza took Renzo Coen Beninfante, a thirty-four-year-old musician from Ancona, by surprise. He was arrested in Dumenza, near Luino. One of his brothers was arrested toward the end of November, in another town on Lake Maggiore, while a third brother was captured in Rome at the end of April 1944. All three brothers were deported to Auschwitz. None returned.

Fleeing Jews were arrested in the border zone on October 12, 16, 19, 25, and 26, some in the Como area, others in the town of Luino: thus began a steady stream of arrests that proceeded doggedly until the Liberation.[2] In the months that followed, Jews from Venice, Verona, Mantua, Bologna, Ancona, and Genoa, from Turin and other towns and villages in the Piedmont region, from Fiume, and from as far afield as Russia, Turkey, and Egypt (that is, these were their places of birth) were arrested in Porto Ceresio, Ponte Tresa, Cremenaga, Pino, Luino, and other small towns in the Varese and Como areas. They were captured as they journeyed toward or neared the border, often double-crossed by the impromptu guides who were supposed to take them to their freedom and who had collected large sums of money from them to do it but instead betrayed and abandoned them to the authorities. Sometimes a single tip could lead to the arrest of several families, as in the case of three families with a total of eleven members ranging in age from eleven to seventy-five apprehended on December 11. A report on the matter by the prefect of Sondrio read: "[They were arrested] in this province to which they had presumably traveled in order to secretly cross the border to Switzerland and avoid internment under the recent provisions."[3] They were incarcerated at Sondrio and Milan before being transferred to the Fossoli transit camp and from there to Auschwitz, from where none of them would ever return.

At the start, in October 1943, Antonio Solinas, the police chief of Varese, had tried to delay handing over the lists of the Jews residing in the town and province to the Germans. After the war he explained to the investigating magistrate that "I found myself faced with the dilemma of either handing over the list against my conscience, as well as against the provisions laid down by the ministry, or refusing to do so. However, I would not have achieved my purpose by refusing because I would have been arrested and the Germans would have obtained the list anyhow." Solinas ended his statement by describing that, at the end of October, "two armed Germans [entered the police headquarters] to take the list of Jews by force" and that, "faced with the force of arms and given that most of the Jews had already fled to safety during the month of October [at least this is what the chief of police claimed], I signed the list and handed it over to the Germans."[4] From that moment onward, usually under the initiative of the German forces (in late December 1943, Franz Stangl, the former chief of the concentration camps of Sobibor and Treblinka, and the Jewish collaborator Mauro Grini both also arrived in Varese), searches were carried out in hospitals, convalescent homes, and religious institutions. At the end of January 1944, the Italian police, acting on the instructions of the GNR of Milan, arrested two Polish Jewish women who had fled from Milan to the Casa San Giuseppe, a local religious institution. When interrogated by the GNR of Varese, one of the women replied, "I am a member of the Jewish race. About thirty-five years ago I left Poland to settle in Austria. Following the expulsion decree of the Austrian government, I moved to Italy. [. . .] My husband (also a foreigner of the Jewish race) has been interned in the concentration camp of Civitella del Tronto (near Teramo) for about three and a half years. After the last bombing in Milan I fled to Arcisate." The police confiscated 3,125 lire, a coin purse, ration cards, and bread vouchers from her and 8,000 lire, a suitcase containing clothes, and personal possessions from her companion. Both were deported to Auschwitz about two months later; neither would return.[5]

Guides generally demanded between five and ten thousand lire per person to accompany people across the border, although the fee could rise to forty thousand if the route was particularly difficult. They could double their earnings by betraying their clients: they would pocket the fee as well as the reward for turning them in. The testimonies of those who survived describing their experiences tend to reveal a similar pattern of events: "My mother paid 10,000 lire per person, that is, for me and my father who had already left. [. . .] As we walked toward the border, our guides began to whistle as if to give a signal. Then one of them admitted to me that he was a spy [. . .]. They made us sit down on the banks of the Tresa river near Cremenaga [. . .]. Then Italian soldiers came and arrested us. The guides had a friendly conversation with the Guardia di Finanza agents [. . .]. The next morning the Germans came for us."[6]

However, there are other cases—I do not here address successful attempts to expatriate[7]—when the Guardia di Finanza (whose agents were called *finanzieri*) offered Jews protection. For example, a Jew who was hidden with his family in the Osteria Del Vecchio, a tavern on Mount Bisbino, near Como, routinely played cards with the soldiers from the neighboring barracks. "One day, the Jews just disappeared," related the rather hostile report, "quietly reaching Switzerland [. . .] thanks to their friendship with the *finanzieri*."[8] Another contemporary source also describes how the *finanzieri* "responsible for patrolling the borders [. . .] would, for a handsome sum, abandon their posts just as the refugees were crossing the border."[9] Sometimes the money extorted from fleeing Jews did guarantee their salvation. On other occasions, if they were unable to make the additional payments demanded by their guides, refugees might be forced to turn back, often with tragic consequences. This was the case of the "Aryan" Angelo Balcone, his Austrian Jewish wife, Edvige Epstein, their "mixed-blood" four-year-old son, Gabriele, and their Austrian Jewish friend Luisa Schlesinger. The guide who had agreed to take the two women and the child from Luino to the border in early December 1943 asked them for a further ten thousand lire in addition to the thirty thousand he had already received. Unable to meet his demands, they spent the night in a hotel in Germignaga where they were joined by Edvige's husband. The following day, Angelo noticed "two men in plainclothes on bicycles who looked at him with undeniable interest while nodding at each other": they were both Public Security agents—a vice-brigadier and a border guard from Luino. "I continued watching them as they headed for the Trattoria del Ponte, [where Balcone's family and friend were hiding] left their bicycles at the door, and, looking quite sure of themselves, marched inside. It was only then that I realized that we had fallen into a trap. I returned to find my loved ones with the two policemen who were asking for their documents. We were identified as Jews attempting to flee to Switzerland and asked to accompany them to the Luino police station."[10] Angelo was soon released as an "Aryan," while his son managed a daring escape, helped by the clergy and thanks to a faked appendicitis. Edvige and Luisa were imprisoned and deported: only Edvige returned from the camps.[11] Forty years later, she gave her version of those events: "On the following morning [after turning back from the border], as we were walking toward the car, we were met by two *carabinieri*, who took us straight to the SS office. After I fearfully asked one of the *carabinieri* what would happen to us, he replied, I know as much as you do! [. . .] Later we heard a rumor that there was a reward of 2,000 lire for every Jew handed over to the Germans."[12] They were probably betrayed by the owner of the hotel where they had spent the night.

A postwar trial held at the Varese Court of Assizes confirmed the existence of a "criminal pact" between inside men, guides or smugglers, and border guards (there were eleven accused) that had led to the betrayal and arrest of sixty or more Jews, only three of whom survived deportation to the extermination camps. The verdict delivered against the group, which had enjoyed the trust of the provincial branch of the National Liberation Committee (which headed the anti-Fascist Resistance), included the description of a "typical" episode. The victim, a lawyer called Segre, "soon noticed the suspicious behavior of [his guide], who lied to him, claiming that they had already reached the border after only a short stretch, when the border was still distant. [The guide] told Segre to proceed by himself toward a certain locality, saying that there he would have found himself in Switzerland." But the lawyer, sensing a trap, refused to proceed and returned to Luino, where he "stopped off in a tavern. Soon after, [the 'recruiter,' i.e., the person who had connected Segre with the guide] appeared, immediately making a hasty departure, only to be replaced by the border guards, who promptly arrested Segre." In 1947 all those involved were given sentences ranging from as little as five to a maximum of twenty years. But by 1952, thanks to commutations and pardons, they had all been released.[13]

Most often it was therefore double-dealing guides who betrayed and condemned their clients in order to make a quick profit. And those arresting and robbing prisoners were, after all, executing an order and applying the law—albeit often also for reasons of self-interest. In other cases, however, ideologically motivated executioners surfaced. This was clearly the case of the Second "Monte Rosa" Legion of the Border Police of the National Republican Guard, which, in December 1943, informed the prefect of Como about its activities intended to strike the "Judaic parties usually concealing valuables and assets stolen from the Nation's wealth in their ragged loot." Between early October and December 12, 1943, the "Monte Rosa" Legion arrested fifty-eight Jews, proudly describing their operations as follows: "The Jews fleeing to the border in an attempt to reach the hospitable Swiss soil—a refuge for rabbis—and to elude the solemn and providential Fascist laws are thwarted by the tireless patrols of the GNR who track all paths, even the most risky, in every kind of weather and at all hours, voluntarily extending their shifts, to uncover the dark and threatening activities of these cursed sons of Judas."[14] Sometimes, to justify them, the Italian executioners would triumphantly tout their actions.

Eight

A City without Jews

Brescia

"December 2, 1943. Following the announced measures for the internment of Jews in concentration camps, yesterday six police squads were charged with rounding up and arresting all persons of the Jewish race residing in Brescia, while the *carabinieri* were issued an urgent request to arrest the Jews residing in the province." This report by the Brescia chief of police, Manlio Candrilli, confirmed the immediate execution of the order for the arrest of Jews that had been issued by the Ministry of the Interior. In the weeks and months that followed, twenty-six of the fifty-six Jews officially residing in Brescia were imprisoned, transferred to the Fossoli transit camp, or delivered directly to the Germans and deported to their deaths. On the day before the first arrests, the local newspaper *Brescia Repubblicana* commented: "Today's police order regarding the Jews will be met with great satisfaction by all those Italians (and they are undoubtedly the best) aware of the subversive actions carried out by the Jews against the unity and honor of our Country."[1] This blend of ideological pride and rancor came from a city in northern Italy not far from the capital Salò or from the other

political and military command centers of the Fascist Social Republic. Brescia appears in this chapter as an example of the ordinary administration of the persecution
of Jews in a city that was virtually "without Jews"[2] and
that, in any case, would have become so following the
arrest of a few dozen Jews and their families.

Already in October 1943 the prefect of Brescia had
asked the police headquarters to provide him with the
list of "Israelites residing in the provinces of Brescia and
Cremona to be passed on to the German Command,"
which had requested it. Now the Italians, thanks to this
same list, could take the initiative independently. Among
the first Jews to be arrested in Brescia were a father and
son, Guido and Alberto Della Volta. Guido had been
taken to police headquarters for verification, and Alberto
had offered to take his place, perhaps fearing that they
were going to send his father to a labor camp in Germany or "draft" him for civilian forced labor in Italy.
Instead they were both taken into custody. Guido, originally from Mantua, was a pharmaceutical business-
man in his late forties who had, for a long time, played a
prominent role in the life of the town where he was also
the commissioner of the Fascist provincial trade union of
chemical product merchants. He had been unaffected
by the first racist measures of 1938 because his mother
was Catholic. His sons had continued to pursue their
schooling, and the eldest, twenty-one-year-old Alberto,
had even started his university studies. But in the spring
of 1939 and later in February 1942, Della Volta was first
"reported" and then officially classified as belonging to
the "Jewish race." He had been denounced by his business partner, who had considered it his "duty" to inform

the prefecture, police headquarters, and the Provincial Council of Corporations that Guido Della Volta was "believed to be of the Jewish race." Nevertheless, at the time of his arrest, the chief of police noted that, until that moment, Guido had continued to play "a leading role in the management and administration of the company." Two months after their incarceration in Brescia by the Italian police, father and son were transferred to Fossoli. On February 22, 1944, they left for Auschwitz on the first transport to leave the Italian camp.

Initially assigned to work duties, in October 1944 Guido was sent to the gas chamber, while Alberto did not survive the death marches that followed the evacuation of the Polish extermination camp in January 1945. He left behind a friend, Primo Levi, who had fallen ill with scarlet fever and had therefore remained in the camp infirmary. Primo would write about him in *If This Is a Man*, in *The Periodic Table*, and in other publications, describing him as "my friend Alberto." In the meantime, only a few days after the arrest of Guido Della Volta, "after a long discussion" the partners of the Pharmaceutical Chemical Consortium, the business formerly headed by Guido, decided to "continue running the company as has been done so far, until such a time as the appropriate authority clarifies the situation of [their] partner." He would, however, be replaced, at least temporarily, by a former partner—the very man who had reported him in 1942. Only a few weeks later, that partner was replaced on the board of the consortium by a representative of the Republican Fascist Party. In the meantime, the stocks belonging to Della Volta and his wife, Emma Viterbi, who had managed to escape arrest by fleeing from Brescia with her younger son Paolo, had been sequestered in various banks. While in January 1944, the furnishings of their apartment were "given for the use" of the "German Political Gendarmerie based in Brescia" by means of the usual detailed yet arbitrary bureaucratic acts of spoliation. Della Volta's car, a Fiat 1500, which had been taken by the director general of the Office of Exchange and Currency for his own personal use, was returned to the Chemical Consortium in the summer of 1944 at the instruction of the prefect. Another apartment owned by the family was plundered. Their lakeside villa near Desenzano, which had been requisitioned on behalf of the Ministry of National Defense in September 1943, was handed over to a brigadier of the local Carabinieri command, who had—in the words of the report filed on behalf of the Della Volta family after the war—"stripped" the building "with the help of his lover." The villa had then been occupied by officials working at the nearby Republican Fascist military airport.[3]

The reminiscences of this political prisoner represent one of the few firsthand testimonies about the incarceration of a number of Jews in Brescia: "I was taken to a cell where an elderly man called Benghiat was being held; I later learned that he was Jewish and that he had been a professor at the Paris Sorbonne. He was a lovely person, a man of exquisite tact who was of great help to me as I adjusted to the shock [of imprisonment]. [. . .] I spent only a few days with Professor Benghiat, before he was taken away, I later found out, to Carpi [i.e., the transit camp of Fossoli, near Carpi]."[4] The Jews of Brescia were arrested thanks to the zealous response to Chief Candrilli's orders by the police, *carabinieri*, and GNR. The same chief of police informed the prefect about the arrests, describing in detail events involving Jews who were residents or property owners in the small towns throughout the province: "On the 12th of this month, the aforementioned Raul Natan and his brother Assalone were arrested in Calvagese della Riviera for belonging to the Jewish race [. . .]. I hereby inform you that at the time of the arrest the sum of 2,428 lire was confiscated from Natan, and 2,000 lire from his brother Assalone. The command of the Bedizzole Carabinieri station carried out the sequestration of all of the furniture found in their home, which has been itemized in the enclosed list."[5] In another communication Candrilli writes: "On the 21st of this month, at the request of this Office, the Carabinieri Command station of Remedello arrested the following for belonging to the Jewish race: Said Lusena son of the late Ernesto, age fifty-five, from Livorno, who is an office worker, and his sons, Piero, age twenty-six, from Alexandria (Egypt), who holds a degree in chemistry, and Silvio, age twenty-four, from Alexandria (Egypt), who is an agricultural consultant. The Command found no money, furniture, or valuables in their home, only the total sum of 803.30 lire on their persons and the objects listed in the report."[6] On December 31, in Tignale Brescia, the Italian gendarmes arrested Maurizio Benghiat, born in Smirne, Turkey, on January 19, 1881: we already know him from the testimony about his incarceration in Brescia.[7] The above-named Jews were all sent to Auschwitz; none would return.

Both the police headquarters and prefecture often took action in response to tips, reports, and information, sometimes received from anonymous sources and documented in reports like the following one sent to the police headquarters by the prefectural commissioner of Borgo San Giacomo. It stated: "Elisa Ascoli, daughter of Simone, believed to be a resident of Milan, Jewess, owns a watermill and a little over 2 hectares of adjoining land in this municipality." This information had been uncovered thanks to the bureaucratic and investigative diligence of the commissioner and his staff: "Ascoli was never a resident in this municipality and her status as a Jew actually surfaced when files were being compiled on her sons, Graziano and Livio Levi, sons of the late Primo." After establishing that Elisa Ascoli resided in Milan, the chief of police immediately contacted his colleagues there to ensure that they had acted in accordance with the law: "I therefore ask for confirmation that Ascoli resides there and either that she has been arrested in compliance with the racial laws or that your office has issued a warrant for her arrest."[8] But Elisa had already left Milan in August 1943.

At the request of the mayor of Mairano, the local police headquarters had asked for the intervention of the *carabinieri* of Dello, a small town in the vicinity: "We have been informed that a Jewess named Ines Jarak is a resident in Mairano and that she also owns property in the said locality. We hereby request that your station takes steps to ascertain whether Ines Jarak still resides in Mairano, and, if the answer is in the affirmative, to carry out her arrest and transfer her to prison making her available to this office." Suspicions about the presence of Jews in Desenzano led to the following demand to the GNR in March 1944: "We have been informed that the son of a certain Mortera Levi, otherwise unknown, Jew, is a resident in this locality and owns property in the area."[9]

Sometimes such reports contained indications or suggestions—evidently issued authoritatively—concerning measures to adopt: "Giulio Lenghi, proprietor of Apollonio & C. and the person responsible for collecting signatures calling for the replacement of the Era Fascista [a statue celebrating Fascism] in Piazza della Vittoria after July 25, [1943, the day of Mussolini's toppling]. He has come to ask for the recognition of his exoneration documents[10] to ensure that neither he nor his son are treated as Jews. It is definitely necessary to sequester both his printing shop and his stationery store and to have them managed by an administrator," reads a note with an illegible signature that is dated December 19, 1943. A few weeks later, after the flight of the proprietor, a representative of the Apollonio staff submitted a report to the prefect accusing the current firm's director of being under the controlling influence of the fugitive owner: "As you well know, the Jew [Lenghi] has been removed in practice; but do not believe that we have extirpated Judaism because his influence continues under Damiano Guizzon, the technical director [. . .], a tormenter loyal to a wicked Jew. Even more Jewish than the fugitive proprietor, he is also an undesirable person." The report accused the director of anti-Fascism, despotism, and corruption, insisting upon his subjection to the Jewish owner: "All that matters to him are the miserly interests of the fugitive Jew, although he has not neglected his own interests or failed to line his pockets, while ensuring that he has enough funds to maintain the fugitive Jew abroad

along with his worthy relatives." The Apollonio printing shop, which had been sequestered and confiscated
in January 1944, went on to print, among other publications, the *Gazzetta Ufficiale*, the official series in which the
Polygraphic Institute of the Republic of Salò published
its laws and decrees, including those ordering the confiscation of Jewish property.[11]

Sometimes, of course, reports could prove baseless.
In the spring of 1944, a GNR commandant transmitted a tip regarding a Mr. Loewenthal to the police station, which promptly initiated an investigation, only to
discover that the allegations were unfounded. In fact,
despite Mr. Loewenthal's surname, described by the station as being "utterly Jewish," and his hasty departure
"without further news and leaving behind his property,"
Mr. Loewenthal, upon his arrest and interrogation, was
able to produce a birth certificate and baptism certificate
bearing the same date, thus proving that he did not belong to the "Jewish race."[12] Sometimes Italian and German persecutors could also find themselves at odds, as
in the case of the Loewy sisters, Carola and Helene, who
were born at Gardone Riviera in 1914 and in 1916, re-
spectively. The local German and Italian administrations
disagreed on how to deal with these young women, who
were daughters of a baptized foreign Jew from Mora-
via and an "Aryan" mother of "Germanic nationality."[13]
After being arrested with their father in early December 1943 and incarcerated by the *carabinieri* of the town
of Salò, the Loewy sisters were released on January 21,
1944, "at the request of this prefecture, undoubtedly at
the behest of the German authorities," as the chief of police of Brescia wrote with some irritation in his report. In

fact, the German authorities had been persuaded to get involved by the girls' mother, the aforementioned German national. Their father, Massimo Loewy, aged sixty-four, who had been baptized as a Protestant in Frankfurt almost forty years earlier, submitted a request to the prefect of Brescia in February 1944 asking to be released on grounds of age and because he had been living in Italy for several decades. Although his daughters had been freed, Massimo was transferred to the Fossoli camp barely a week after submitting his petition. Fifteen days later he was deported to Auschwitz and never returned.

Nine

INFORMING

No one has been more acute than Hannah Arendt and Primo Levi in describing collaborationism as a consequence of the moral decay produced by the upside-down world of deportation and extermination.[1] Levi, in particular, describes the space where executioners and victims meet as the "gray zone." Before attacking the existence of the individual in order to wipe out that of the entire group, genocide sweeps away all the rules of civil coexistence, tearing apart the fabric of social and even family relations. One of the most perverse aspects of the encounter—and the clash—between executioners and victims is informing, which pits even victims against each other. This final chapter describes some of the darkest and most painful episodes in the period leading up to the extermination of the Jews. Informing was a pervasive phenomenon involving hundreds of ordinary Italian men and women, who betrayed their own fellow citizens by denouncing them for profit, revenge, perfidy, or even political conviction. As mentioned before, informing is one of the keystones of civil war. It always concerns our closest, even intimate, neighbors and can be considered an indirect cause of violence to which it is all the easier to accede because the actual violence that results will take place elsewhere, at a later date.[2]

The ranks of the Italian executioners included a number of Jewish victims who would also play a role in bringing about the genocide. One such informant was Mauro Grini, a Jew from Trieste whose name is sadly etched into the memory of the Jewish communities, although many have preferred to consign his name and activities to oblivion. Grini epitomizes how this type of violence can insinuate itself into ordinary, everyday relations, breaking the standards and norms of coexistence and playing out in unpredictable ways. Between the spring and the summer of 1944, he left Trieste for Venice, where he settled in a hotel near the railway station. Grini, who had an office in the local SS command, was on a mission to find Jews from his home city who had fled to the lagoon city where they hoped not to be recognized. A number of them had also gone there because the city was not being bombed and, although crowded, resources were not lacking in what was one of the leading cities of the RSI. Grini had with him a list of potential addresses to check and could count on information from the police. He carried out a door-to-door search of hotels, boardinghouses, and inns, carefully checking their guest registers. He would also lurk in strategic places in a city where, despite its labyrinth of back alleys, the main roads on which people moved, the major crossings, and public transportation routes were controlled easily enough by monitoring the city's entry and departure points. For example, after Liberation, Teresa Pescatori pressed charges at the Venice police headquarters, describing how Grini had caused her husband and brother-in-law, Ignazio and Adolfo

Luft, Jews of Polish origin, to be arrested on the train going from Venice to nearby Mestre "with the collaboration of the railway [police]."³ After arresting them, the Italians had handed them over to the Germans.

Grini had used the same tactics in Trieste and would do the same for a brief time in Brescia and, finally, in Milan, where, in March 1945, he appeared in the bulletin published by the Corpo Volontari della Libertà (the Resistance's Freedom Volunteer Corps). In it, he was described under one of his many names:

> Grun from Trieste. A Jew, he calls himself Grini, Verdi or Doctor Manzoni. He works for the German SS, and specializes in capturing fellow Jews whose acquaintance he has previously made. [...] He has contributed to the arrest of around three hundred Jews in Trieste, a hundred or so in Venice, and in Milan he catches an average of two a day. His father, a well-known tailor, is in Trieste, in a concentration camp. Grini earns seven thousand lire for every Jew he helps arrest. In Milan he is always accompanied by two Germans, strolling about with them in the city center, especially in the Galleria [a busy shopping mall]. He is tall, elegantly dressed, aged thirty-five or thirty-six, with brown hair beginning to thin at the temples and a pronounced Semitic nose.⁴

After the war Arturo Friedman, a Jew from Fiume who had fled to Venice, described the arrest of his father-in-law, Simeone Levi, after an encounter with Grini in the center of town. In August 1944, Levi was stopped "by a man whose appearance corresponded to a description of Mauro Grini, whom he did not know." Against his family's warnings to lie low, during yet another outing he bumped into Grini again. This time the encounter would lead to Levi's arrest. A few days later, Friedman happened to glimpse his father-in-law on a waterbus on the Grand Canal. He was just about to approach him when he saw that Levi was in the company of two unfamiliar men. He later learned that they had taken his father-in-law to his apartment and then to the Santa Maria Maggiore prison. A few days later Simeone Levi was transferred to Trieste, where his family "lost every trace of him." Friedman was later told by his father-in-law's maid that Grini had paid a visit to the apartment, "accompanied by a German, and had grabbed everything he could get his hands on (clothes, jewels, money, etc.)." In his statement Friedman also gave the names of four other persons, three women and a man, who had been denounced by Grini.[5] The encounters that had led to the denunciation were therefore casual, and the victim was arrested by plainclothesmen on public transportation, in broad daylight.

In a letter written in the spring of 1946 to the Jewish Community of Trieste, Egon and Walter Sussland, who had taken refuge in Venice, reconstructed Grini's modus operandi: "He would stroll through Venice, and upon meeting an acquaintance, would greet him and then continue on his way. But he was obviously being followed by a tail responsible for shadowing the acquaintance in question, who would let down his or her guard after seeing Grini walk off. This system sought to ensure that there was no risk that others would go underground after the first arrest. In fact, after expressly broadcasting his intentions, Grini would leave Venice for a few days, then return unexpectedly to ensnare his victims." Grini used this method to identify and arrest several Jews from Trieste, including Signor Carlo Macerata, who was seized "in Campo San Bartolomeo," a square in the heart of the city, near the Rialto Bridge. A few days later, Grini went to the prison where he roughed up Macerata to extract information from him about his belongings before going to his apartment and stripping it bare. Egon Sussland knew a *questurino*—an agent working at police headquarters—who claimed to have "shadowed people for Grini." This confirms that Grini worked in tandem with another Italian who helped him shadow and inform on people in exchange for a fee. The Susslands had been told by a Canadian acquaintance who happened to be at a party also attended by Grini that Grini had "drunkenly [confessed] to receiving seven thousand lire for every captured Jew, in addition to a fixed monthly fee of ten thousand lire, and to responsibility for the arrest of at least 1,400 people to date."[6] These figures were probably inflated, but if we consider the arrests attributed to Grini by the bulletin published by the Milanese Resistance and the fact that a number of the arrests involved entire families, it is likely that his victims numbered in the hundreds.

According to a report from November 1944, Grini would often approach people, especially shopkeepers, on the mere suspicion that they were Jewish (if they had a Jewish-sounding surname, for example), also targeting anyone he knew to be wealthy, with the specific intention of robbing them. He would force his victims to give him information about any other Jews among their acquaintances. The same source mentioned a certain "Dr. Iasonni" at the police headquarters who "took orders" from Grini—possibly the police agent mentioned above—calling him a "top-notch scoundrel." The source also claimed that a German officer had told police commissioner Andriulli that Iasonni had spoken of Grini in the following way: "when Grimm [*sic*] has finished his assigned search for the Jews . . . he then drew his fingers across his own throat as if to hint that they would have him killed."[7]

In the spring of 1947 the Milan Court of Assizes convicted Grini of collaborationism: "Grini Mauro Graziadio, son of Samuele and of Cornelia Coen Luzzatto, born in Trieste on June 4, 1910, [is hereby sentenced] to death by firing squad."[8] It is likely, however, that Mauro Grini was already dead by then, killed at San Sabba, the transit and extermination camp created and run by the Germans in Trieste.[9] The system of informing, which entailed the collaboration of other victims involved in the hunt for Jews, as well as the support of other police forces or staff, would end in the death of the informants themselves once they had outlived their usefulness or if they dared breach the rules of collaborationism.

Another notorious case of Jewish collaborationism involved Celeste Di Porto, an eighteen-year-old Jewish girl of humble origins living in the Roman ghetto. Di Porto's lover was a member of the Fascist squad led by the former World War I elite soldier Giovanni Cialli Mezzaroma, who was in league with the German police. This squad patrolled the capital responding to tips and sequestering Jewish property.[10] It used Celeste's insider knowledge of Rome's Jewish community to find Jews who had previously avoided arrest. With Celeste's help, the Fascists identified their victims through patrols and chance encounters. On one occasion, during lunch in an osteria in the city center, Celeste spotted a party of Jews that included women and children; shortly afterward the entire group was arrested. In other cases she would accompany the Fascists to their victims' homes or cruise around in a car with these tormentors searching for Jews on the streets of Rome. Or she would frequent places—like the Porta Portese market—where Jews would still publicly engage in business in order to scrape together enough money to survive. No one was safe from her, not even her own family, who were arrested along with other Jews living in the same apartment block in the ghetto.[11]

Celeste Di Porto remains tragically impressed on the memories of many Roman Jews.[12] A typical episode is recounted in the testimony of Gabriella Ajò: "One day my mother went to Portico d'Ottavia and came home crying because she'd seen Stella [one of Celeste's nicknames] Di Porto walking arm-in-arm with Fascists and Nazis. She was extremely beautiful, only nineteen, and her father turned himself in to the Nazis for the shame of having a daughter who was an informer."[13] According to another victim, "My father was taken at the Porta Portese market, where he went because we had to eat, and he used to go out there to work. He was denounced by Celeste Di Porto and left on the last transport to Auschwitz."[14] Informing, particularly when it takes place within a community, shatters the rules of everyday living and of familiarity, ripping apart the fabric of social relations. People needed to eat and therefore work, and our witness describes how her father, while trying to satisfy these primary needs, was denounced, arrested, and sent to his death. Such betrayals break the relationship of mutual trust and the unspoken rules of belonging: "Another one of these fascist informers was Celeste Di Porto: a true disgrace. When we used to go out, if we happened to meet other Jews, we would pretend not to know each other, because you never knew, we were afraid of being discovered so we never told anyone where we lived."[15] Just greeting someone or being greeted could prove fatal: "We got along just fine until one day there was a knock on the door—it was March 21, 1944: the Fascists had received a tip. When we got to Fossoli, we realized that we had probably been denounced by the so-called 'Black Panther,' Celeste Di Porto. I had no idea who she was, but my mother knew her and once we were at Fossoli she remembered that, a few days earlier, she had bumped into [Celeste] at Porta Pia and that, during the course of their conversation, she had told her that she was hiding at grandad's."[16]

However, informing was mainly carried out by hundreds of non-Jewish Italians who grasped at the chance to make money, exact revenge, or remove an obstacle in their professional or personal sphere. A huge number of arrests and sequestrations or confiscations of property were carried out thanks to denunciations made both in person and anonymously. It is not war alone that turns men and women against their neighbors, it is also civil war—by definition a violent, fratricidal clash—as well as a context of genocide that identifies an enemy within, declaring them to be inferior and alien, authorizing their persecution, and legitimizing their victimization. Even those not actively involved, those without particular ideological ties, find themselves living in and adhering to a new system of norms that imposes—and in any case authorizes—the use of violence even against next-door neighbors, acquaintances, or friends. In this context personal motivation, private hate, and the hope of making a quick profit can surface.

In 1943–45 voluntary denunciation was incentivized and even structured by a police system that relied on informers to pursue its persecutory ends and to extend involvement and joint responsibility for violent acts to ever-wider areas of society. The search for support and complicity in the genocidal situation increased the number of executioners—albeit with differing degrees of responsibility. When questioned after the war, Bruno Pastacaldi, a stage designer turned Jew hunter and torturer who worked at the Florentine Office of Jewish Affairs, described the daily steady stream of tips: "Every day the post brought anonymous reports of the whereabouts of Jewish families. The office secretary gave them to Martelloni, who would stamp them, then pass them on to me for further checks. Often I would go to the address indicated only to find the SS there or that they had already been there and gone. Evidently these anonymous reports were also being sent to their command."[17] The polycratic reality of civil war, of reborn Fascism, and of the German occupation led to an increase in the number of recipients of these reports and in the number of corresponding persecutory initiatives.

Sometimes clerks would denounce their office manager, a maid or farmworker would denounce an employer—in which situations social redress likely played a part—or business associates would denounce their partners. Sometimes old quarrels would resurface, while others were motivated by the hope of seizing their victim's property. As already mentioned, informers were entitled to a reward: up to five thousand lire for every reported Jew, less in the case of women and children.[18] The accounts of survivors often describe a situation in which long-standing relationships of absolute trust were brutally betrayed. Sometimes students would denounce their teachers or even betray their own classmates. According to historian Osti Guerrazzi, in two such cases the informers were ideologically motivated, or, at a minimum, ideology played a role in precipitating the possibly vindictive violence of informing. A sixteen-year-old from Rome, known for his commitment to the Fascist Federation, denounced his Jewish music teacher, Professor Roberto Valabrega, even planting a Communist flyer in his briefcase. On no less than two occasions—in November 1943 and January 1944—Valabrega was arrested by the Fascists as he left his student's home after a lesson: the second time proved fatal and ended with his deportation. The other case took place in February 1944, when a young man named Umberto Spizzichino arranged to meet a classmate, hoping for some comfort before fleeing to Switzerland, only to find the SS waiting for him; Spizzichino was arrested and deported while his "friend" would later fight for the Nazis, earning the sobriquet "the Hangman."[19] Sometimes "Fascist beliefs," "underlying antisemitism," and "utilitarian reasons" would overlap,[20] as in the case of a *squadrista* in Florence, who denounced his mother's tenant, a deaf elderly woman, when his relationship with her soured. Old age or ill health: nothing mattered; in fact, sometimes when the elderly or sick were involved, people seemed to feel a greater detachment and lack of pity, a kind of fatalism.

While the reasons for informing may sometimes remain obscure, we have to assume that informant and victim were often close, if not intimately close. Such a relationship may have occasioned the arrest in Rome of Giulio Levi, who had escaped the German roundup of October 16, 1943. An anonymous typewritten letter was sent to the police headquarters of Rome in mid-February 1944, ungrammatically reporting that

> the Jew Giulio Levi, son of Raffaele, residing at Via Passeggiata Ripetta no. 16–19 where he still has his home, which he claims has been damaged, has sought refuge in the home of the Lelli family, at Via Filippo Corridoni n. 19–2, stairwell F. The Jew Giulio Levi goes by the name of Edmondo Carletti, son of the late Desidarato and Agostina Rocchi, born on April 19, 1921 at Olevano Romano [...]. In fact, this Carletti has family living at Olevano Romano at the above address but has been a prisoner since the invasion of Sicily, and like a true Jew has managed to get hold of an identity card and ration cards since he has been in the town, as have his relatives still living there [...]. I swear that this is the truth. My respects.

A couple of days later Giulio Levi (aka Edmondo Carletti) was arrested and taken to the prison of Regina Coeli. In April he was transferred to Fossoli and was later deported to Auschwitz, where he died. After the war, the woman who had informed on him was placed on trial, having been accused by Giulio's father, but was acquitted on the grounds of insufficient evidence.[21]

In Milan, as in Rome and Venice, Fascists would prowl around the city in search of Jews or tips. An entry in a diary of the period states: "The thugs of the fascist republic drive around the streets of Milan with their guns out, in search of Jews. They are offering a reward of nine thousand lire for every Jew handed over, even for children [...]. They board all trains, go into porters' lodges, where they make agreements to share their earnings." The collaboration of porters, which had flourished during the twenty-year Fascist regime, was essential for control of the territory and vital to the overall system of informing. In November 1943, a police lieutenant and a plainclothes agent with the badge of the "Piazza Colonna political command," the headquarters of the Republican Fascist Party, entered a building on Viale Mazzini. They forced the porter to tell them which apartment belonged to a certain Gastone Coen, then stole various goods from it. "As they left, they ordered the porter to telephone the Political Office in Piazza Colonna if the Coens returned."[22]

Often a tip was followed by a surprise ambush in the street. One day, while in Turin, Roberto D'Ancona, who was hiding in a house on a nearby hill, was stopped on the tram by a man identifying himself as a Public Security agent accompanied by two other men. The agent had evidently received a tip informing him about D'Ancona and the fact that he had hidden a stash of money to cover his costs while living underground. After accompanying him to his home and threatening to take him to police headquarters, the agent forced D'Ancona to hand over his money. On this occasion D'Ancona managed to escape arrest, but he was not so lucky the next time, a few months later, when a group of Italians and Germans came for him in a farmhouse in the Piedmont country-side. From there he would be deported to Auschwitz and then to Dachau, where he would die.[23] Without excluding the materialistic and career-driven motivations, through which Fascism had flourished, historian Luciano Allegra has suggested that in the Italian Social Republic "the hunt for the Jew was part of an animus, a deeply internalized worldview that reduced the enemy—whether real or presumed—into a pariah, investing the holder of power with the right of life and death without appeal."[24]

Conclusion

Amnesties, Repression, and Oblivion

In Giacomo Debenedetti's short story *Eight Jews*, Public Security police commissioner Raffaele Alianello testifies at the trial of Rome's chief of police, Pietro Caruso. Shortly before being questioned, just as the judges are attempting to reconstruct the role played by the Italian police at the Ardeatine massacre, Alianello ponders to himself: "What we must quickly produce, deftly imply, is verifiable evidence, proving that while the wicked collaborated with the 'Nazi-Fascists,' we [the Italian police] were among the good." "The problem is basically very simple," reflected the commissioner, "what was black yesterday is now white, and vice versa. What was the trademark characteristic on the calling card of Fascism? What are the fingerprints of Fascism? Darn it, the persecution of the Jews. And consequently what is the most incontrovertible characteristic of anti-Fascism? The protection of the Jews."[1]

Debenedetti's account reveals already in the fall of 1944 his awareness of the widespread and strategic tendency—mainly by the actors themselves—to recast the role of the Italian executioners in the 1943–45 persecution of the Jews, starting with the police forces. After the war, no one was ever put on trial for participating in Fascism's antisemitic policies: neither the 1938 anti-Jewish policy nor the policies introduced by the Italian Social Republic. In only a handful of cases were such responsibilities even included among minor charges. In general, the persecution of the Jews was not considered a crime or a specific offense, nor was it even considered an aggravating factor for other crimes. This happened in the larger context of an underestimation of the culpability of Italian Fascism during the twenty-year period and during the Salò period.

The main provisions leading to the trial and subsequent pardon for Fascist crimes were in the Legislative Decree of July 27, 1944, no. 159, enacted by the Bonomi government and identifying crimes carried out during the dictatorship, and the presidential decree of June 22, 1946, no. 4, better known as the "Togliatti amnesty" (after the Communist leader and Minister of Justice Palmiro Togliatti), which annulled most of these crimes. The 1944 decree punished those who committed violent acts in the name of Fascism, those who created and later helped consolidate the Fascist government and dictatorship, and finally those who "collaborat[ed] with the invading Germans" after September 8, 1943. The 1946 amnesty decree applied to convictions for military and political crimes that had required sentences of up to five years' imprisonment, and also extended to crimes such as massacre, plunder, and destruction of property, to civil war, and to collaborationism. (The previous provision of April 1945 had placed in this category all roles with a political responsibility: from ministers to presidents of Special Courts, from Fascist party officers to newspaper editors.) Almost 10,000 of the 13,000 people who had either already been convicted or who were still on trial at the beginning of the summer of 1946 were granted amnesty.[2] They included numerous Fascist leaders such as Giuseppe Bottai, Luigi Federzoni, and Carlo Scorza—even though the majority enjoyed remissions or commutations of their sentences. Others were able to use extenuating circumstances, received particularly light sentences, or were acquitted on the basis of hasty, lenient, or ideologically constrained judgments. The same magistracy responsible for passing judgment on Fascist crimes was not subjected to judgment and operated continuously from the Fascist regime onward, so the judges and magistrates in office during the 1920s and 1930s remained at their posts after the war.[3]

Even if we limit ourselves to the racist policies of Fascism, it becomes clear that within the magistracy itself figures who had been directly involved in applying racist legislation went on to enjoy distinguished careers after the war. For example, Carlo Alliney, chief of staff at Giovanni Preziosi's General Inspectorate of Race and a consultant for racial legislation to the RSI government, later became attorney general in Palermo and then an appellate court judge.[4] We must also mention Gaetano Azzariti, former president of the Tribunal of Race from 1938 to 1943, who became minister of justice under Badoglio's government in the summer of 1943, before being appointed head of the Legislative Office at the Ministry of Justice under the Togliatti government, ending his career as president of the Italian Constitutional Court in the 1950s.[5] Another government figure who succeeded in being cleared of all charges was Domenico Pellegrini Giampietro, who went from undersecretary of finance during the final months of the Fascist regime to finance minister of the RSI, in which position his responsibilities included the confiscation of Jewish assets. Pellegrini, who generously financed both the reestablished Fascist party and the Germans by dipping into the Italian state coffers, was described in his acquittal as a "courageous unwavering opponent" of the Nazis.[6] In fact, often no specific guilt or responsibility was attributed to those who played a public role in the RSI. This was either because they were considered representatives of a "Sovereign State that was politically and legally organized" and, as in the case of the acquittal of a judge, invested with the power of jurisprudence by that State or because the German occupation had crippled that State's "political and administrative autonomy" (as was ruled in the case of a prefect).[7]

The failure to recognize acts connected to antisemitic persecution, as specific crimes, completely undermined the gravity of that policy and, as in the case of other crimes of the Fascist period, created a "fact-finding vacuum,"[8] especially at the judicial level. A partially analogous situation unfolded in the postwar, international scene at the Nuremberg trials, in which the detailed and unprecedented intentions and nature of the crimes of the Holocaust received much less attention than crimes against peace and war crimes, which dominated the proceedings. The legal and judicial approach—and even more frequently the lack of justice—was among the first steps to reducing, concealing, and canceling Italian responsibility for antisemitic racism and the subsequent genocide of the Jews. This weakened the overall condemnation of Fascism and contributed to shaping the positive and benevolent vision of Italians that gained credence after

the war and still often prevails today thanks to the intervention of other long-term factors. In fact, Minister of
Justice Togliatti underscored the need for the "reconciliation and pacification of all good Italians"[9] in a report in-
troducing measures that pardoned those who committed
Fascist crimes, literally anticipating the term "good Italian." This term was later used by historians, who wrote
about the "myth of the good Italian."

This individual and collective removal of Italian responsibility took place not only at the judicial level but
on multiple other levels: political, military, diplomatic,
and historiographic, as well as in memoirs. The Ministry
of Foreign Affairs, for example, deliberately promoted
the reduction or negation of Italian responsibility in anti-
Jewish policies by preparing documents that pointed out
and often exaggerated (by decontextualizing) the protection of Jews by the Italian army in the south of France
and in the Balkans until July 25, 1943 (the end of Mussolini's regime). It also did so by intervening with regard
to the documentation of Fascism's anti-Jewish policy in
the Italian peninsula and how it was to be portrayed.[10]
For example, in the fall of 1945, an Italian ambassador
urged the government to send him documents "clearly
showing that not only were Italian initiatives concerning
race involuntary but their formal character ceased [that
is, they were enforced] only when the German invaders
extended their direct control over the application of antisemitic measures."[11] The minister of the interior transmitted these same instructions to the Italian prefectures
almost like guidelines for the collection of information
on persecution in Italy. "The instinctive spirit of tolerance and the kindheartedness" of Italians toward the

Jews in the Italian occupied zones were highlighted by the international press of the time—such as the *New York Times*—and even by the first authoritative non-Italian historiography to be published.[12] In the immediate postwar period, this positive and rather naïve vision of Italian behavior was accepted and supported—and sometimes even generated—by the same Italian Jewish elite. On the one hand, the reduction of Italy's responsibility by the Jews answered the need for the reconciliation and assimilation of Jews in the Italian society that had just welcomed them back; on the other, it expressed the sincere gratitude of those who had been saved from deportation. At another level, there was a tendency to whitewash the co-responsibility of many Jews who had supported the Fascist regime until 1938. Their co-responsibility was fundamentally identical to that of most Italians. It has been observed that the attitude of many Italian Jews toward the extermination was "a complex interweaving of repression and commemoration. The monumentalization of the memory of the genocide, with the condemnation of the German people, and the repression of Italian responsibilities as regards antisemitism could coexist."[13] Massimo Adolfo Vitale, head of the Research Committee on Jewish Deportees (set up by the Jewish Communities), was decidedly a lone voice in the wilderness when, in the fall of 1947, he claimed: "After the Armistice [of September 8, 1943], the courageous people who ignored the dangers to save some Jews were not lacking, but there were few of them, while the police agents together with the *Carabinieri*, in almost all the cases, carried out the work of reporting, arresting and transferring to the internment and death camps. We have gathered vast documentation relating to this, documentation covering all the Italian regions."[14] Still, over a decade after the end of the war, in December 1956, the president of the Union of Italian Jewish Communities referred to the 1943–45 period in the following terms: "Everyone had done their utmost; all [. . .] were careful to warn the doomed innocent victims; all the friends, the acquaintances, the neighbors were ready to take them in, to hide them, to help them; they all rushed to provide the Jews with false documents and to divert the searches." As historian Guri Schwarz commented, "What perhaps is more disquieting is that such words were quoted by historian Renzo De Felice, from the first [1961] to the last [1993] edition of his book *The Jews in Fascist Italy: A History*, in order to maintain the thesis of a collective Italian opposition to German extermination policy."[15] This was one of the main historical works by an author who was for many years the authority on Italian Fascism. Promoted by the Jewish Communities, De Felice's work influenced several decades of the historiography on antisemitism and the persecution of the Jews. The image of Italian benevolence and generosity—as opposed to that of the "wicked German"—was at the heart of the judicial, diplomatic, political, and historiographic interpretations of the behavior of the Italians that gradually became a deeply rooted stereotype. These stereotypical and mainstream portrayals would intensify in later years—paradoxically in the 1980s, just as the awareness of the Holocaust was on the rise in both Europe and Italy—through mass media products such as Nicola Caracciolo's documentary *Il coraggio e la pietà* (Courage and Compassion). In the words of its author, this television documentary was intended to show how the Italians had remained "immune to that awful [. . .] 'psychological epidemic' of antisemitism, at least in its murderous Nazi variant." The 1990s and early 2000s were characterized by a variety of educational programs, journalistic books, and television series like the one dedicated to the "Righteous" Giorgio Perlasca (an Italian Fascist who apparently rescued scores of Jews in wartime Budapest). The underlying message of such reconstructions was that "where venal collaborators elsewhere colluded to deport Jews, by contrast Italians, whether neighbors, friends, priests and nuns, or indeed Fascist officials, diplomats or soldiers, did all they could, in private and behind the scenes, to save 'their' Jews."[16]

In the context of the reconstructions and historical judgments that tended to recast the Republic of Salò as a regime under occupation without any decision-making autonomy, there was all the more a natural inclination to present the anti-Jewish policy as German imposed. Historians tended to downplay the matter of antisemitism and its ideological and political radicalization,[17] and it was also minimized or even denied in the memoirs of those who had participated in the RSI.[18] Even war criminals like General Mario Roatta, commander of the Italian Second Army in the Balkans, attempted to rebrand themselves as saviors of the Jews. In his memoirs, which grossly inflated the numbers of Jews who were not handed over to the Germans in Croatia (and of the Serbs saved from the Ustaša), Roatta, who was responsible for antipartisan repression and brutalities against the civilians in this area, described the Italian occupation as benevolent and humanitarian.[19] Over the past two decades or so, the figure of the savior, of the "Righteous," has become so influential[20] that at times people have been described as saviors, though they played no such role, while the merits of others have been inflated or even largely fabricated. This is what happened in the case of the deputy commissioner of Fiume, Giovanni Palatucci, whose role in saving hundreds of Jews is now being seriously questioned.[21] The recognition and appreciation of the Righteous have often been precisely linked to an idyllic and stereotypical portrayal of the Italian character. In fact, the official publications of Yad Vashem, the Holocaust Museum in Jerusalem responsible for awarding the title of Righteous, have insisted on the supposed Italian rejection of antisemitism starting from 1938 because it was "contrary to Italian traditions," on the "huge wave of solidarity," and on the "charitable spirit" toward the Jews after the armistice of September 8, 1943. These qualities and attitudes were cast as permanent collective attributes of the Italians. However, historian Liliana Picciotto, one of the leading authorities on the Shoah in Italy, has pointed out that the investigations carried out by Yad Vashem to recognize the Righteous "lack the support of serious historical research."[22]

The increasing attention paid to the Italian Righteous, whose numbers have quadrupled during the past twenty years—from 120 cases in 1994 to 568 in 2013[23]—seems to be connected to the growing focus of the collective memory on the saviors at the expense of the executioners or, in other respects, to the forfeiture of the memory of politically militant forms of resistance in a post-ideological era. In Italy's case this has been further reinforced, since

2000, by the law that established Holocaust Remembrance Day on January 27. This law explicitly names the saviors while referring to the "extermination," "racial laws," and "persecution" in abstract terms, without specifically mentioning those responsible or those who carried out these acts.[24]

The aim of this book is to offset such tendencies by placing the executioners at the forefront. By way of conclusion I would like to mention the fate of some of them in the postwar period. Giovanni Preziosi, one of the most fanatical ideologues, committed suicide with his wife on April 25, 1945, when the infernal world that he had envisaged and desired had finally collapsed. Giocondo Protti, the fierce antisemitic propagandist, went back to his clinical practice and to his hobbies of writing and painting. Giovanni Martelloni, director of the Office of Jewish Affairs in Florence, who was responsible for rounding up Jews, was put on trial in 1950 while still a fugitive, along with sixty-seven other accused persons, many of whom had worked in his office (having been members of his "gang," as they said at the time). All the defendants were acquitted of the crime of collaboration owing to an intervening amnesty or insufficient evidence.[25] In Rome, police chief Pietro Caruso was tried, sentenced to death, and executed by firing squad just a few months after the liberation of the capital. The spy Celeste Di Porto was tried for collaboration and was not eligible for a pardon because her crimes involved financial gain: Di Porto was sentenced to twelve years, later reduced to seven.[26] In Venice, Deputy Commissioner Mario Cortellini, one of the heads of the Race Office of the Venice Police, who had supervised most of the seizures of Jewish property, was not only acquitted but even put in charge of the Office for the Recovery of Jewish Property in the same police headquarters after the Liberation. As a result, an expert in seizures, who had also been responsible for making door-to-door arrests, was the very person tasked with returning these assets to the Jews who had been his victims.[27] I have not been able to discover the fate of Filippo Cordova, the Venice chief of police who gave the order for the first roundup of Venetian Jews in December 1943, because his file was checked out from the Italian Central State Archives in 1983 by the State Police Personnel Office and never returned.[28]

Despite the activities of the Anselmi National Investigation Commission on the Spoliation of Jewish Assets—set up over half a century after the events concerned—we have yet to see an explicit assumption of responsibility or any self-critical gestures or amends by the Italian state, whose police forces and administrations contributed directly to the genocide of the Jews. On Holocaust Remembrance Day, or on similar occasions, there is rarely any specific mention of the roles and responsibilities of the thousands of Italians who all played varying but crucial parts in the tragic process that resulted in genocide. The only exception is an unavoidable and hasty mention of the racial laws of 1938, and occasionally an allusion to collaboration with the Germans—or more frequently the use of the rhetorical, inaccurate, and partially exonerating term "Nazi-Fascists." In many aspects Italy has moved from the "era of the witness,"[29] which placed the victims' experiences and memories in the spotlight, to what we could term an "era of the savior" celebrating the rescuers. In so doing, it has bypassed the "era of the executioner," which would have necessitated an examination of the misdeeds of the past—which have now faded into guilty oblivion.

Acknowledgments

This book is first and foremost an ethical and political gesture intended to direct the attention of public opinion and historians to the role of the Italians in the genocide of the Jews, one of the most tragic chapters of the Fascist experience, one that I believe Italian society has yet to fully process. I am referring to Italy's failure to fully come to terms with its complex political and moral responsibilities in regard to Fascism, and with their implications and consequences.

I wish to thank the two people who provided the most encouragement for this project: David Bidussa and my wife, Giulia Albanese. I am also grateful to the people who have, over the years, given me the opportunity to discuss the topics of my book with them: in particular, Enzo Traverso, Marie-Anne Matard-Bonucci, and Marcello Flores (also for having invited me to teach at the Master in Human Rights and Genocide Studies at the University of Siena), in addition to Michele Sarfatti and Liliana Picciotto Fargion, from the CDEC Foundation of Milan. I would like to thank all of my colleagues and fellow researchers quoted in every chapter, because without their indispensable studies and research I would never have written these pages. I would also like to thank those who have invited me to conferences or seminars, giving me the opportunity to present materials now included in this book. I am grateful for having had the privilege of attending the lectures and seminars held at UCLA by one of my mentors, Saul Friedländer, who introduced me to the historiography of the Holocaust. Another mentor, who taught me to study the enemy, was Mario Isnenghi. I'd also like to thank my friends Alberto Cavaglion and Ernesto De Cristofaro for reading my manuscript and offering me their criticism and advice. The responsibility for what I have written rests only with me.

For the Italian edition of the book, I would like to thank Mattia de Bernardis at Giangiacomo Feltrinelli Editore. For the English-language edition, thanks go to Fred Appel at Princeton University Press, Robert Gordon, and Abigail Green; to Oona Smyth and Claudia Patane for the translation; and to David I. Kertzer for his generous preface.

This book is dedicated to my daughters, Sara and Lea, in the hope that they will grow up in a country that is more aware of its past and, therefore, more free.

Notes

Prologue

1. For the anti-Jewish persecutions in Venice, see *Gli ebrei a Venezia, 1943–1945: Una comunità tra persecuzione e rinascita*, edited by Renata Segre (Venice: Il Cardo, 1995). For the concert and football match, see accounts in the local press: *Il Gazzettino*, December 5 and 6, 1943. For information on the blackout and weather conditions, see *Il Gazzettino*, November 16 and 22, 1943.

2. See Carlo Fumian, "Venezia 'città ministeriale' (1943–1945)," in *La Resistenza nel veneziano: La società veneziana tra fascismo, resistenza, repubblica*, edited by Giannantonio Paladini and Maurizio Reberschak (Venice: Comune di Venezia, 1985), 365–94.

3. *Il Gazzettino*, April 1 and 6, 1944, quoted in *Gli ebrei a Venezia*, 170.

4. See Raphael Lemkin, *Axis Rule in Occupied Europe* (Washington, DC: Carnegie Endowment for International Peace, 1944), chapter 9.

5. An entire field of studies has grown up in the overlap between law, history, and the social sciences. For an overview of this approach, see *The Oxford Handbook of Genocide Studies*, edited by Donald Bloxham and A. Dirk Moses (New York: Oxford University Press, 2010).

6. For useful clarifications and distinctions with regard to legal definitions and their applicability within a historical context, beginning with the concept of collaboration, see

Anton Weiss-Wendt and Uğur Ümit Üngor, "Collaboration in Genocide: The Ottoman Empire 1915–1916, the German-Occupied Baltic 1941–44, and Rwanda 1994," *Holocaust and Genocide Studies* 25.3 (Winter 2011): 407–10.

7. See Zygmunt Bauman, *Modernity and the Holocaust* (Ithaca, NY: Cornell University Press, 1991), 24, quoting Raul Hilberg, *The Destruction of the European Jews* (New York: Holmes and Meier, 1985), 3:1024. At the same time, following in the footsteps of these authors, other writers have observed that "an army of civil servants performed tasks essential to the final Solution [. . .] however [these tasks] had nothing murderous about them. They became murderous only through being integrated into a global chain culminating in the gas chambers, a chain whose final outcome was not necessarily known to its individual participants." Enzo Traverso, *Fire and Blood: The European Civil War*, translated by David Fernbach (Paris, 2007; London: Verso, 2015), 92.

8. The most detailed and authoritative overviews are by Liliana Picciotto Fargion, *Il libro della memoria: Gli ebrei deportati dall'Italia 1943–1945* (Milan: Mursia, 1991); Michele Sarfatti, *The Jews in Mussolini's Italy: From Equality to Persecution*, translated by John Tedeschi and Anne C. Tedeschi (Turin, 2000; Madison: University of Wisconsin Press, 2006). See also *Storia della Shoah in Italia: Vicende, memorie, rappresentazioni*, 2 vols., edited by Marcello Flores, Simon Levis Sullam, Marie-Anne Matard-Bonucci, and Enzo Traverso (Turin: UTET, 2010). The leading studies on the role of the Italian executioners are represented by the essays and documents collected in *Ebrei in Toscana tra occupazione tedesca e RSI: Persecuzione, depredazione, deportazione (1943–1945)*, 2 vols., edited by Enzo Collotti (Rome: Carocci–Regione Toscana, 2007); and Amedeo Osti Guerrazzi, *Caino a Roma: I complici romani della Shoah* (Rome: Cooper, 2005).

9. Mimmo Franzinelli, *L'amnistia Togliatti: 22 giugno 1946: Colpo di spugna sui crimini fascisti* (Milan: Mondadori, 2006), 51.

10. At the level of narrative, this account aims to draw upon the now classic works on the history of the Shoah for the way in which they manage to focalize its intertwinement of "utter criminality" and "utter ordinariness"; see Saul Friedlander, *Nazi Germany and the Jews*, vol. 1, *The Years of Persecution, 1933–1939* (New York: Harper Collins, 1997) (who refers with such terms to the "dynamics" of the Nazi regime); Christopher Browning, *Ordinary Men: Reserve Police Battalion 101 and the Final Solution in Poland* (New York: Harper Perennial, 1992); and Jan T. Gross, *Neighbours: The Destruction of the Jewish Community in Jedwabne, Poland* (Princeton: Princeton University Press, 2001).

Chapter One

1. On Italy's civil war, see Claudio Pavone, *A Civil War: A History of the Italian Resistance*, translated by Peter Levy and David Broder (London: Verso, 2014).

2. On Fascism and antisemitism, Renzo De Felice's classic work has not lost its relevance: *Storia degli ebrei italiani sotto il fascismo* (Turin: Einaudi, 1993) (see also *The Jews in Fascist Italy: A History*, translated by Robert L. Miller [New York: Enigma Books, 2001]). Michele Sarfatti has provided a new slant to these studies, emphasizing the early development of Fascist antisemitism in *The Jews in Mussolini's Italy*. Marie-Anne Matard-Bonucci has attempted to reconcile these approaches in *L'Italia fascista e la persecuzione degli ebrei* (Paris, 2007; Bologna: Il Mulino, 2008). Giorgio Fabre claims that Mussolini had always been an antisemite in *Mussolini razzista: Dal socialismo al fascismo: La formazione di un antisemita* (Milan: Garzanti, 2005).

3. See De Felice, *Storia degli ebrei italiani*, 141–48, 206–10; Sarfatti, *The Jews in Mussolini's Italy*, 95–108; Annalisa Capristo, "L'esclusione degli ebrei dall'Accademia d'Italia," *La rassegna mensile di Israel* 67 (2001): 3, 1–36; and Simon Levis Sullam, *Una comunità immaginata: Gli ebrei a Venezia (1900–1938)* (Milan: Unicopli, 2001), 64n59.

4. Gianluca Gabrielli, "Un aspetto della politica razzista nell'impero: Il 'problema dei meticci,'" *Passato e presente* 15, no. 41 (1997): 77–105.

5. Giorgio Fabre, *L'elenco: Censura fascista, editoria e autori ebrei* (Turin: Zamorani, 1998).

6. *Gli ebrei a Venezia 1943–45: Una comunità tra persecuzione e rinascita*, edited by Renata Segre (Venice: Il Cardo, 1995), 97.

7. Simon Levis Sullam, "Gli ebrei a Venezia nella prima metà del Novecento," in *Storia di Venezia: L'Ottocento e il Novecento*, edited by Mario Isnenghi and Stuart J. Woolf (Rome: Istituto dell'Enciclopedia Italiana, 2002), 3:1679.

8. For some examples of this, see *La menzogna della razza: Documenti e immagini del razzismo e dell'antisemitismo italiani*, edited by Centro Furio Jesi (Bologna: Graphis, 1994); and Francesco Cassata, *"La Difesa della razza": Politica, ideologia e immagine del razzismo fascista* (Turin: Einaudi, 2008).

9. On various aspects of the intertwining of anti-Judaism and modern antisemitism in Italy in the nineteenth century, see Simon Levis Sullam, "I critici e i nemici dell'emancipazione degli ebrei," in *Storia della Shoah in Italia*, edited by Flores et al., 1:37–61; on how this process of intertwining evolved in Fascism, see Elena Mazzini, *Ostilità convergenti: Stampa diocesana, razzismo e antisemitismo nell'Italia fascista (1937–1939)* (Naples: Edizioni Scientifiche Italiane, 2013).

10. On betrayal, see Luigi Ganapini, *La repubblica delle camicie nere* (Milan: Garzanti, 1999), 143; Dianella Gagliani, "Violenze di guerra e violenze politiche: Forme e culture della violenza nella Repubblica sociale italiana," in *Cri-*

mini e memorie di Guerra: Violenze contro le popolazioni e politiche del ricordo, edited by Luca Baldissara and Paolo Pezzino (Naples: L'ancora del Mediterraneo, 2004), 294, 306, 314; and Toni Rovatti, *Leoni vegetariani: La violenza fascista nella RSI* (Bologna: Clueb, 2011), 30.

11. Manuel Delgado, "Confini labili: La guerra civile tra individuo e società," in *Guerre fratricide: Le guerre civili in età contemporanea*, edited by Gabriele Ranzato (Turin: Bollati Boringhieri, 1994), 138.

12. Mario Isnenghi, "L'esposizione della morte," in *Guerre fratricide*, 334.

13. Stathis N. Kalyvas, *The Logic of Violence in Civil War* (New York: Cambridge University Press, 2006), 330–36.

14. In this regard we should recall Gross, *Neighbours*, an exemplary study that is part of a wider reflection that has been underway for some time examining the relationship between intimacy and genocide in the Shoah and in other genocidal contexts.

15. Mary Douglas, *Purity and Danger: An Analysis of Concept of Pollution and Tabu* (1966; London: Routledge, 2003), 5–6. In his reflection on the "extreme dimension, spreading without limits" of civil war, Enzo Traverso has also evoked—with reference to Norbert Elias, not Douglas—its "strong symbolic dimension"; see his *Fire and Blood*, 85–86.

16. The article is included in the appendix of Mauro Raspanti, "L'Ispettorato generale per la razza," in *La Repubblica sociale italiana a Desenzano: Giovanni Preziosi e l'Ispettorato generale per la razza*, edited by Michele Sarfatti (Florence: Giuntina, 2008), 138–39.

17. See Renato Del Ponte, "'La Vita Italiana' di Giovanni Preziosi durante la RSI: Una ricerca storico-bibliografica," in *Giovanni Preziosi e la questione della razza in Italia*, edited by Luigi Parente, Fabio Gentile, and Rosa Maria Grillo (Soveria Mannelli: Rubbettino, 2005), 253–66.

18. See Raspanti, "L'Ispettorato generale per la razza," 131.
19. The memorandum is published in De Felice, *Storia degli ebrei italiani*, 612–19 (the quotation appears on 617). The previous letter from Preziosi to Mussolini, dated December 9, 1943, is quoted in ibid., 454.
20. See Raspanti, "L'Ispettorato generale per la razza," 116–17.
21. Quoted in De Felice, *Storia degli ebrei italiani*, 617.
22. Giovanni F. Martelloni, "Gli ebrei in Firenze," a series of articles published between January and May 1944 and reproduced in *Ebrei in Toscana tra occupazione tedesca e RSI*, vol. 2, *Documenti*, 163–74.
23. "Exonerated" Jews ("ebrei discriminati") were Jews for whom the anti-Jewish measures had been partly alleviated usually for patriotic activities.
24. Giovanni F. Martelloni, "Dalla storia all'attualità: Le conversioni e gli ebrei," *Il Nuovo Giornale*, February 11, 1944, reproduced in *Ebrei in Toscana tra occupazione tedesca e RSI*, vol. 2, *Documenti*, 177–79.
25. Giovanni F. Martelloni, *La confisca dei beni ebraici: Decreto legislativo 4 gennaio 1944–XXII n. 2. Premessa—Testo—Commento* (Florence: Cya Editore [1944], reproduced in *Ebrei in Toscana tra occupazione tedesca e RSI*, vol. 2, *Documenti*, 181–88, quotation on 187).
26. Traces of Protti's activity in 1942 can be found in Archivio di Stato di Venezia, Gabinetto Prefettura, versamento 1956, box 7, file Attività professionali Ebrei. For his ultra-Fascist positions in the final phase of the Fascist period, see, for example, Giocondo Protti, "Teoria e pratica corporative," *Ateneo Veneto* (January–February 1937): 1–4; and Protti, "La dittatura determina le opere dello spirit," offprint from *Italia Nova: Settimanale dei Fasci di Combattimento di Venezia*, September 17–24, 1939.
27. Similar themes also emerge from the article published in installments written by Giocondo Protti, "Israele o Cristo?" *Il*

Solco fascista, Reggio Emilia, January 6 and 10, 1944, quoted in Antonio Zambonelli, "Ebrei reggiani tra leggi razziali e Shoah, 1938–1945," *Ricerche Storiche* 35.91–92 (December 2001): 53.

28. Giocondo Protti, "Il dramma di Israele," *Orizzonti*, single issue (Venice: Edizioni Erre, 1944), 39–43. Protti's interests in hematology and radiology in this period are documented in *La luce del sangue* (Milan: Bompiani, 1945), a medical text containing no references to racial or antisemitic matters.

29. Biblioteca-Archivio Renato Maestro della Comunità ebraica di Venezia, materials from the exhibition *Gli ebrei a Venezia 1943–45: Una comunità tra persecuzione e rinascita* (1995), copy of the document dated April 4, 1944, held in the Yad Vashem Archives, Jerusalem.

30. See Francesco Germinario, "Antisemitismo senza ebrei: I temi dell'attività pubblicistica dell'ultimo Giovanni Preziosi (1943–1945)," in *La Repubblica sociale italiana a Desenzano*, 77–108.

31. The two quotations are in Ganapini, *La repubblica delle camicie nere*, 143.

32. "Tutti gli ebrei in campo di concentramento," *Rivoluzione*, Padua, December 5, 1943, in Mario Isnenghi, "Stampa del fascismo estremo in area veneta: Tracce e reperti," in *Tedeschi, partigiani e popolazioni nell'Alpenvorland (1943–1945)*, proceedings of the Belluno conference (April 21–23, 1983) (Venice: Marsilio, 1984), 131–32. Isnenghi also underlines the strong anti-Jewish sentiment pervading the only surviving issue of *Fiamma Italica: Giornale dei lavoratori e dei combattenti*, published in Vicenza on April 28, 1944 (ibid., 135n16).

33. Matteo Mazzoni, "I nemici della RSI nella propaganda del fascismo toscano," *Italia contemporanea*, no. 224 (September 2001): 450–52.

34. See, for example, *L'Italia in guerra 1940-43: Immagini e temi della propaganda fascista* (Brescia: Fondazione L. Micheletti, 1989), 53-54.

35. Mario Isnenghi, "Autorappresentazioni dell'ultimo fascismo nella riflessione e nella propaganda," in *La Repubblica sociale italiana 1943-45*, edited by Pier Paolo Poggio, *Annali della Fondazione L. Micheletti*, no. 2 (1986): 102-3.

36. Cited in Ganapini, *La repubblica delle camicie nere*, 139 (December 2, 1943).

37. The issues of these newspapers that came out on December 3 and 4, 1943, are both cited by Mayda, *Storia della deportazione dall'Italia*, 147.

38. "Gli ebrei in campi di concentramento," *Il Gazzettino*, December 1, 1943, cited in *Gli ebrei a Venezia*, 151.

39. Cited in Mayda, *Storia della deportazione dall'Italia*, 147.

40. Cited in Matard-Bonucci, *L'Italia fascista e la persecuzione degli ebrei*, 360 (December 1, 1943); see also Enzo Collotti, *Il fascismo e gli ebrei: Le leggi razziali in Italia* (Rome: Laterza, Bari, 2003), 129-30.

41. Cf. Isnenghi, *Autorappresentazioni dell'ultimo fascismo*, 108-10.

42. *Ecco gli ebrei*, Edizioni Popolari, n.p., 1944 (printed November 4, 1944, by the press of *Il popolo vicentino*, Vicenza).

43. See, for all quotations and the full transcription of some of the essays, Paolo Ferrari and Mimmo Franzinelli, eds., "A scuola di razzismo: Il corso allievi ufficiali della Gnr di Fontanellato," *Italia contemporanea*, no. 211 (June 1998): 417-44.

44. Ibid., 431, 433.

45. Francesco Cassata, *"La Difesa della razza": Politica, ideologia e immagine del razzismo fascista* (Turin: Einaudi, 2008).

46. See the section titled "Manifesti murali, volantini, stampati propagandistici illustrate," in *La menzogna della razza*, 198-208, as well as *1943-45: L'immagine della RSI nella propaganda*, edited by the Fondazione Luigi Micheletti (Milan:

Mazzotta, 1995), with an essay by Mario Isenghi, "Parole e immagini dell'ultimo fascismo," 11–41.

47. Cassata, *"La Difesa della razza,"* 356.

48. Quoted in in Ganapini, *La repubblica delle camicie nere*, 139, from the newspaper *La riscossa*, Turin, December 16, 1943.

49. Francesco Germinario, *L'altra memoria: L'estrema destra, Salò, la Resistenza* (Turin: Bollati Boringhieri, 1999), 58–73.

Chapter Two

1. The document is cited and the episode reconstructed by Bruno Maida, *La Shoah dei bambini: La persecuzione dell'infanzia ebraica in Italia, 1938-1945* (Turin: Einaudi, 2013), 137. The reconstruction and documents that follow here are quoted from Osti Guerrazzi, *Caino a Roma*, 129–30. The records of the trial show that the family was probably betrayed by the Jewish collaborationist Celeste Di Porto. See Anna Foa, *Portico d'Ottavia: Una casa del ghetto nel lungo inverno del '43* (Rome: Laterza, 2013), 93–94.

2. The police commissioner "managed to prove that he had acted under duress and that he had actively helped Jews and partisans" according to Foa, *Portico d'Ottavia*, 94.

3. Donald Bloxham, "Organized Mass Murder: Structure, Participation and Motivation in Comparative Perspective," *Holocaust and Genocide Studies* 22.2 (Fall 2008): 203–45, quotes on 207, 216–17; more generally see Donald Bloxham, *The Final Solution: A Genocide* (Oxford: Oxford University Press, 2009).

4. On these aspects, see Zygmunt Bauman, *Modernity and the Holocaust* (Cambridge: Polity Press, 1991).

5. Traverso, *Fire and Blood*, 86.

6. The role played by Italians in the Roman arrests emerges continuously in the eyewitness accounts collected by

Marcello Pezzetti, *Il libro della Shoah italiana: I racconti di chi è sopravvissuto* (Turin: Einaudi, 2009), 73–88. One of the few specialized studies dedicated to this matter is Frauke Wildvang, "The Enemy Next Door: Italian Collaboration in Deporting Jews during the German Occupation of Rome," *Modern Italy* 12.2 (June 2007): 189–204, which claims that around a thousand Roman Jews died in the course of 1944.

7. Some of these questions are inspired by Jacques Sémelin, *Indagare su un massacro*, an appendix to Jacques Sémelin, *Purificare e distruggere: Usi politici dei massacri e dei genocidi* (Paris, 2005; Turin: Einaudi, 2007), 473–76. See also Jacques Sémelin, "Analisi di un crimine di massa: La pulizia etnica nell'ex Jugoslavia (1991–1999)," in *Il secolo del genocidio*, edited by R. Gellately and Ben Kiernan (Cambridge, 2006; Milan: Longanesi, 2006), 443–65.

8. I also found comparative suggestions that helped me formulate these questions in the reconstruction of the French case; see Laurent Joly, *L'antisémitisme de bureau: Enquête au cœur de la préfecture de Police de Paris et du commissariat général aux Questions juives (1940–44)* (Paris: Grasset, 2011); and Jean Marc Berlière, *Policiers français sous l'Occupation* (Paris: Perrin, 2009).

9. The reconstruction here and in the previous paragraph is based on Massimiliano Griner, *La "Banda Koch": Il Reparto speciale di polizia, 1943–44* (Turin: Bollati Boringhieri, 2000), in particular, 97 and 99 for the quotations; 33 for the number of arrests.

10. See Caruso's circular to local police stations dated February 24, 1944, quoted in Liliana Picciotto Fargion, *Il libro della memoria: Gli ebrei deportati dall'Italia 1943–1945* (Milan: Mursia, 1991), 874.

11. Maida, *La Shoah dei bambini*, 136.

12. The episode has been reconstructed from the trial records in Roberta Cairoli, *Dalla parte del nemico: Ausiliare, delatrici e*

spie nella Repubblica sociale italiana (1943-1945) (Milan: Mimesis, 2013), 81–87.

13. On the widespread policing method adopted in the RSI in the twenty years of Fascism, see Luciano Allegra, *Gli aguzzini di Mimo: Storie di ordinario collaborazionismo (1943-1945)* (Turin: Zamorani, 2010), 172, as well as Mimmo Franzinelli, *Delatori: Spie e confidenti anonimi: L'arma segreta del regime fascista* (Milan: Feltrinelli, 2012).

14. The episode, described by its protagonists, Evelina and Bianca Montefiore, is told in Liliana Picciotto Fargion, *Gli ebrei in provincia di Milano: 1943/45: Persecuzione e deportazione* (Milan: Fondazione Centro Documentazione Ebraica Contemporanea, Province of Milan, 2004), 51–52.

15. Both documents are reproduced in *La menzogna della razza: Documenti e immagini del razzismo e dell'antisemitismo italiani*, edited by Centro Furio Jesi (Bologna: Graphis, 1994), 337–38. For these developments from September 1939 onward, see Mario Toscano, "L'internamento degli ebrei italiani 1940-1943: Tra contingenze belliche e politica razziale," in *I campi di concentramento in Italia: Dall'internamento alla deportazione (1940-1945)*, edited by Costantino Di Sante (Milan: Franco Angeli, 2001), 95–112.

16. The documents (the last one dated January 14, 1941) are quoted in *La menzogna della razza*, 339–40.

17. This project was identified and reconstructed in *La menzogna della razza*, appendix 3, pp. 369–71. There are also vague mentions of it in Giuseppe Mayda, *Storia della deportazione dall'Italia 1943-1945: Militari, ebrei e politici nei lager del Terzo Reich* (Turin: Bollati Boringhieri, 2002), 149.

18. Quoted in Sarfatti, *The Jews in Mussolini's Italy*, 188, 378n57; see also U. Alfassio Grimaldi, *La stampa di Salò* (Milan: Bompiani, 1979), 51.

19. "Provvedimenti allo studio per la questione ebraica," *La Gazzetta di Venezia*, November 4–5, 1943, reproduced in *Gli*

ebrei a Venezia, 150. For the *Regime fascista* (November 5, 1943), *Corriere della Sera*, and *La Stampa* (November 6, 1943), see Sarfatti, *The Jews in Mussolini's Italy*, 188, 377n54.

20. Mayda, *Storia della deportazione*, 144.

21. On Buffarini's meeting with the prefects and the praise of the Germans, see Luciana Rocchi, "Ebrei nella Toscana meridionale: La persecuzione a Siena e Grosseto," in *Ebrei in Toscana tra occupazione tedesca e RSI*, vol. 1, *Saggi*, 287, 285.

22. Dianella Gagliani, "Violenze di guerra e violenze politiche: Forme e culture della violenza nella Repubblica sociale italiana," in *Crimini e memorie di guerra*, edited by Luca Baldissara and Paolo Pezzino (Naples: L'ancora del Mediterraneo, 2004), 298–99.

23. Quoted in Luigi Ganapini, "Le polizie nella Repubblica sociale italiana," in *I campi di concentramento in Italia*, 288.

24. Ibid., 269–92.

25. Gagliani, *Violenze di guerra e violenze politiche*, 301–2, 312.

26. This is the analysis put forward by Dianella Gagliani, "Il partito nel fascismo repubblicano delle origini: Una prima messa a punto," *Rivista di storia contemporanea* 23–24 (1994–95): 1–2, 159–60, along the lines of Emilio Gentile, *Il problema del partito nel fascismo italiano* (1985), now in Emilio Gentile, *La via italiana al totalitarismo: Il partito e lo Stato nel regime fascista* (Rome: La Nuova Italia Scientifica, 1995), 155–201. See also the wider study by Gagliani, *Brigate nere: La militarizzazione del partito fascista* (Turin: Bollati Boringhieri, 1999).

27. Sarfatti, *The Jews in Mussolini's Italy*, 197.

28. The document is quoted in Mayda, *Storia della deportazione dall'Italia*, 149, citing Klaus Voigt, *Il rifugio precario: Gli esuli in Italia 1933–1945* (Florence: La Nuova Italia, 1996), 2:448. The sites considered were the Monigo concentration camp (near Treviso), which had a capacity of 3,500–4,000 prisoners, the Cairo Montenotto concentration camp (near Savona), which could hold a thousand inmates, and lastly

the Bagni di Lucca camp. These existing camps had already been created for prisoners of war.

29. This possibility is hinted at by Mayda, *Storia della deportazione*, 149, who refers to the establishment of a "further six camps."

30. The formula is in the Italian title and at the center of Davide Rodogno, *Il nuovo ordine mediterraneo: Le politiche di occupazione dell'Italia fascista in Europa (1940-1943)* (Turin: Bollati Boringhieri, 2003); the English translation is *Fascism's European Empire: Italian Occupation during the Second World War*, translated by Adrian Belton (Cambridge: Cambridge University Press, 2006); for a comparison with Italian deportation and concentration policies in the colonial and war occupation contexts, see Costantino Di Sante, "Deportazione e campi di concentramento in Cirenaica e in Jugoslavia," *Italia contemporanea*, no. 252-53 (September–December 2008): 547-65.

31. The document, dated December 4, 1943, is quoted by Enzo Collotti, introduction to *Ebrei in Toscana*, 1:20. It also advised the minister to express his satisfaction for the launch of operations by the Italians and to delay the request to hand over arrested Jews for transportation to the "eastern territories," "because it is likely that concentration will take place more smoothly if the transfer to concentration camps will initially appear to be a final solution and not a preliminary step toward [further] evacuation" (ibid., 21). Ten days later Ribbentrop would send a letter to ambassador Rahn expressing this opinion (quoted below).

32. For a recent overview, see Lutz Klinkhammer, "L'occupazione tedesca in Italia e lo sterminio degli ebrei," in *Storia della Shoah in Italia*, edited by Flores et al., 1:433-53. For the context, see Lutz Klinkhammer, *L'occupazione tedesca in Italia, 1943-1945* (Turin: Bollati Boringhieri, 1993).

33. Picciotto Fargion, *Libro della memoria*, 815, 892n68.

34. For the two episodes, see ibid., 818, 823.

35. Ibid., 796, 815.

36. This is the reconstruction in ibid., 808–10 (for the parallels with Vichy, see 796).

37. Letter of December 14, 1943, cited in Picciotto Fargion, *Il libro della memoria*, 842.

38. See in this regard the documentation emerging from *San Sabba: Istruttoria e processo per il lager della Risiera*, 2 vols., edited by Adolfo Scalpelli (Milan: ANED, 1988).

39. For the Fossoli camp, I base my descriptions on Liliana Picciotto, *L'alba di colse come un tradimento: Gli ebrei nel campo di Fossoli 1943-44* (Milan: Mondadori, 2010).

40. Report to the Research Committee on Jewish Deportees presented by Bruno Fiorentini, December 27, 1945, included in the appendix to ibid., 139.

41. Picciotto, *L'alba di colse come un tradimento*, 41.

42. Ibid., 44.

43. Letter of February 19, 1944, cited in ibid., 46.

44. Report to the Research Committee for Deported Jews, 138.

45. The request and reply both date to January–February 1944; Picciotto, *L'alba di colse*, 263–64.

46. For the quotation and numbers, see Picciotto, *L'alba di colse*, 50, 54.

47. According to Picciotto Fargion, *Il libro della memoria*, 37, in at least four cases (see also the quote by Primo Levi in the opening pages of this book). Reference has also been made to an escort made up of "Fascist elements" based on the findings of Picciotto Fargion and on the testimony of a survivor (Mayda, *Storia della deportazione*, 188–89).

48. Picciotto, *L'alba ci colse*, 107–11.

49. For these episodes, see Mayda, *Storia della deportazione*, 216–18; and Picciotto Fargion, *Il libro della memoria*, 764.

50. All the data in this paragraph are taken from Picciotto Fargion, *Il libro della memoria*, and therefore date to the year of the book's publication (1991); the following edition of 2001 does not update the data. Picciotto's reconstruction does not take full account of the fact that Italian forces were a constant presence—albeit in varying numbers—during the arrests.

51. The percentage of victims out of the total population of Italian Jews does not change the definition of the Italian Shoah as genocide, because the definition of genocide relates to the existence of a project and should not be established in quantitative terms. Nor can we use the percentage of survivors as a basis for judgments on the attitude or, even less so, the national character of Italians.

52. This emerges very clearly from the research in *Ebrei in Toscana tra occupazione tedesca e RSI*, vol. 2, *Documenti*, containing essays that add considerable detail to the information in the *Libro della memoria*.

Chapter Three

1. Michele Sarfatti, *Gli ebrei nell'Italia fascista: Vicende, identità, persecuzioni* (Turin: Einaudi, 2000), 245n47.

2. Ibid., 247n53; see also Ganapini, *La repubblica delle camice nere*, 139. For antisemitism in Roman Fascism, see Amedeo Osti Guerrazzi, *"La repubblica necessaria": Il fascismo repubblicano a Roma, 1943-44* (Milan: Franco Angeli, 2004), 53–62.

3. "Exonerated" Jews were those for whom anti-Jewish measures had been partly alleviated, usually for patriotic activities.

4. Quoted in Giuseppe Mayda, *Storia della deportazione dall'Italia 1943-1945: Militari, ebrei e politici nei lager del Terzo Reich* (Turin: Bollati Boringhieri, 2002), 143.

5. Dianella Gagliani, "Violenze di guerra e violenze politiche: Forme e culture della violenza nella Repubblica sociale italiana," in *Crimini e memorie di Guerra: Violenze contro le popolazioni e politiche del ricordo*, edited by Luca Baldissara and Paolo Pezzino (Naples: L'ancora del Mediterraneo, 2004), 294; Toni Rovatti, *Leoni vegetariani: La violenza fascista nella RSI* (Bologna: Clueb, 2008), 31.

6. See Sarfatti, *The Jews in Mussolini's Italy*, 381n74.

7. Quoted in Mayda, *Storia della deportazione*, 143.

8. According to the reconstruction by Luciana Rocchi, "Ebrei nella Toscana meridionale: La persecuzione a Siena e Grosseto," in *Ebrei in Toscana tra occupazione tedesca e RSI*, vol. 1, *Saggi*, 295.

9. Ibid., 285.

10. For these matters and the documents mentioned, see ibid., 260, 287.

11. See also letter sent by Prefect of Grosseto to Directorate General of Public Security, November 24, 1943, ibid., 287.

12. For this episode and relative documents, see ibid., 309.

13. Ibid., 298. In 1949 Ercolani was sentenced to twenty-one years of imprisonment by the Court of Appeal of Perugia, which made no specific reference to his anti-Jewish actions. He served only a short part of his sentence (ibid., 295n257).

14. See ibid., 278–79.

15. Ibid., 283–84.

16. Valeria Galimi, "Caccia all'ebreo: Persecuzioni nella Toscana settentrionale," in *Ebrei in Toscana tra occupazione tedesca e RSI*, vol. 1, *Saggi*, 192.

17. Ibid.

18. Ibid., 200.

19. Ibid., 196.

20. Ibid., 202.

21. Ibid., 203.

Chapter Four

1. Presidency of the Council of Ministers–Department for Information and Publishing, *Rapporto Generale della Commissione per la ricostruzione delle vicissitudini che hanno caratterizzato in Italia l'attività di acquisizione dei beni dei cittadini ebrei da parte di organismi pubblici e privati* (Rome: Istituto Poligrafico e Zecca dello Stato, 2001), 95 (hereafter *Rapporto* 2001). The commission was headed by Tina Anselmi.
2. Ibid., 100.
3. Ibid., 102.
4. Ibid., 104.
5. Ibid., 107.
6. Ibid., 116, 118, 121.
7. Details of these episodes from the morning reports of the Central Police Station of Rome dated October 19 and November 25, 1943, have been published in ibid., 123.
8. Ibid., 135, 137, 140. These are just a few episodes from the dozens described in ibid., 128–42. For a further description of the confiscations of Jewish property in Tuscany, see the section "Le razzie patrimoniali," edited by Valeria Galimi, in *Ebrei in Toscana tra occupazione tedesca e RSI*, vol. 2, *Documenti*, 201–63, which documents the activities of the Monte dei Paschi di Siena Bank, EGELI's Tuscan head office from 1939 onward.

Chapter Five

1. Telegram, Venice Head of Police Cordova to all Public Security stations, December 1, 1943, in Archivio di Stato di Venezia (hereafter ASV), Gabinetto Prefettura, versamento 1956, box 7, file Anno 1943, Varie. My access to the ASV documents referred to throughout this chapter

was kindly facilitated by Alessandra Schiavon, following authorization by the archive director, Raffaele Santoro, and I would like to thank them both for their help. I have based my description of these Venetian events on the reconstruction in *Gli ebrei a Venezia*.

2. The launch of the deportation process is reconstructed with supporting documents in *Gli ebrei a Venezia*, 151–56, from which my quotations are taken.

3. Telegram, Venice Head of Police Cordova to all Public Security stations and for reference to the Head of the Province and Carabinieri Group, December 28, 1943, in ASV, Gabinetto Prefettura, versamento 1956, box 7, file Anno 1943, Varie.

4. See undated and unsigned typewritten document (1951?) "Relazione per la Signora Fano" (Report for Mrs. Fano), in Archivio Fondazione CDEC, Milano, Comunità Ebraiche in Italia, 1.2.2.1., box 4, file Venice (formerly: AG-13B, Venezia), from which all of the following quotations are taken.

5. Copy of letter from Girolamo Segré to Giuseppe (Pino) Segré, December 1943, in Archivio della Comunità ebraica di Venezia (hereafter ACEV), Fondo Paolo Sereni, serie Deportazione e antisemitismo (currently being reorganized). Girolamo, his wife, Lea Rita Calimani, and their daughter Nedda were all deported to Auschwitz from Fossoli in February 1944 and killed on their arrival in the camp (see Picciotto, *Il libro della memoria, ad nomen*).

6. The assistant chief of police sent a circular dated January 30, 1944, to the head of the Aosta province (we do not know if this made reference to previous general directives) ordering that "Jewish minors should follow the course of their respective families" (quoted in Sarfatti, *The Jews in Mussolini's Italy*, 193).

7. Telegram of the Venetian police headquarters to the management of the Fossoli concentration camp, quoted in *Gli ebrei a Venezia*, 155.

8. Liliana Picciotto Fargion, *Libro della memoria: Gli ebrei deportati dall'Italia 1943–1945* (Milan: Mursia, 1991), 854.

9. Giuseppe Fano to Raffaello Levi, president of the Jewish community in Venice, April 15, 1967, in ACEV, Fondo Paolo Sereni, serie Deportazione e antisemitismo. The archives also hold a copy of the typewritten report by Laura Fano Jacchia, "Fine degli ebrei degenti nei vari ospedali, manicomi, ospizi di cronici, case di salute di Venezia (1944–45)," dated July 1951. On the arrest of Giuseppe Fano and his family, and their encounter with Stangl and Grini at the Ospedale Civile, see the memoir of his wife, Letizia Morpurgo Fano, *Diario: Ricordi di prigionia*, published under the support of the Jewish community of Venice, Tipo-Litografia Leghissa, Trieste, [1966].

10. ASV, Gabinetto Prefettura, versamento 1956, box 5, Ebrei CRA-FIL, file Fano Elena ved. Corinaldi di Emanuele. On the fate of Elena and her brothers, Giuseppe and Giulio Fano, see Picciotto Fargion, *Il libro della memoria*, 261–62.

11. Cannaregio Police station to Venice Police Headquarters, May 3, 1944, ASV, Gabinetto Prefettura, versamento 1956, box 4, Ebrei Cap.-Coz., file Castelnuovo Bice fu Enrico.

12. See exchange of information between San Marco police station and Venice Police Headquarters, March 31 and April 16, ASV, Gabinetto Prefettura, versamento 1956, box 4, Ebrei Cap.-Coz., file C. N. di C.

13. Head of Province of Venice to Venice Chief of Police, March 6, 1944, ASV, Gabinetto Prefettura, versamento 1956, box 4, Ebrei Cap.-Coz., file Cesana Amalia.

14. Mirano *carabinieri* station to the Carabinieri company of Mestre, March 19, 1944, in ASV, Gabinetto Prefettura,

versamento 1956, box 5, Ebrei CRA-FIL, file Errera Paolo, National Republican Guard. The information about the arrest of the Erreras following the report of an informer and about the driver and goods handlers being Italian comes from the interrogation of Napoleone Andriollo carried out at the Venice Police Headquarters, August 22, 1945, ASV, Gabinetto Prefettura, versamento 1956, box 5, Ebrei CRA-FIL, file Errera Paolo (aggiunto). Napoleone and his brother Luigi worked as Italian interpreters at the German command in Venice (see also interrogation of Luigi Andriollo, August 24, 1945, ASV, Gabinetto Prefettura, versamento 1956, box 5, Ebrei CRA-FIL, file Errera Paolo [aggiunto]).

15. National Republican Guard to Carabinieri station Mestre.

16. Conservative sequestration record drawn up by Venice Police Headquarters, April 11, 1944, ASV, Gabinetto Prefettura, versamento 1956, box 5, Ebrei CRA-FIL, file Errera Paolo (aggiunto).

17. Mirano police agent command to Venice Police Headquarters, July 12, 1944, ASV, Gabinetto Prefettura, versamento 1956, box 5, Ebrei CRA-FIL, file Errera Paolo (aggiunto).

18. Chief of Police of Venice to the Prefecture of Venice, July 1, 1944, ASV, Gabinetto Prefettura, versamento 1956, box 5, Ebrei CRA-FIL, file Errera Paolo (aggiunto).

19. Interrogation of Amedeo Vincenti by the Office for the Restitution of Jewish Property (Ufficio Recupero Beni Ebraici) of the Venice Police Headquarters, July 26, 1945, ASV, Gabinetto Prefettura, versamento 1956, box 5, Ebrei CRA-FIL, file Errera Paolo.

20. Report of theft filed by Vittorio Fano at the Police Headquarters of Venice, August 11, 1945, in ASV, Gabinetto Prefettura, versamento 1956, box 5, Ebrei CRA-FIL, file, Fano Vittorio.

21. Statement made by Antonio Tomasella at the Police Headquarters of Venice, Office for the Restitution of Jewish Property (Ufficio Recupero Beni Ebraici), December 15, 1945, ASV, Gabinetto Prefettura, versamento 1956, box 5, Ebrei CRA-FIL, file Fano Vittorio.
22. Interrogation of Tommaso Guerrieri by the Office for the Restitution of Jewish Property (Ufficio Recupero Beni Ebraici) of the Police Headquarters of Venice, September 1, 1945, ASV, Gabinetto Prefettura, versamento 1956, box 5, Ebrei CRA-FIL, file Fano Vittorio.
23. Statement made by Antonio Tomasella.
24. Interrogation of Tommaso Guerrieri by the Office for the Restitution of Jewish Property (Ufficio Recupero Beni Ebraici) of the Police Headquarters of Venice, September 27, 1945, ASV, Gabinetto Prefettura, versamento 1956, box 5, Ebrei CRA-FIL, file Fano Vittorio.
25. Statement made by Antonio Tomasella.

Chapter Six

1. Report drawn up by Vittorio Frilli, secretary of the Jewish community, on July 27, 1944, quoted in Marta Baiardi, "Persecuzioni antiebraiche a Firenze," 53–54. This chapter is based on the study by Baiardi, one of the foremost works of research into the action of the Italian executioners.
2. Report made to the Jewish community of Florence by the sister of his wife, Virginia Gallico (husband and wife shared the same surname), August 22, 1944, quoted in Baiardi, "Persecuzioni antiebraiche a Firenze," 56.
3. Baiardi, "Persecuzioni antiebraiche a Firenze," 62.
4. Ibid., 69–70.
5. Ibid., 73–74.

6. Ibid., 78–79.

7. The report, dated January 13, 1945, is quoted in ibid., 73.

8. Baiardi, "Persecuzioni antiebraiche a Firenze," 77.

9. Ibid., 103.

10. Ibid., 106.

11. Ibid., 111.

12. Ibid., 107.

13. Ibid., 109.

14. Ibid., 131.

15. Statement, July 5, 1947, ibid., 138.

16. Ibid., 136–39.

Chapter Seven

1. Franco Giannantoni, *Fascismo, guerra e società nella Repubblica sociale italiana (Varese 1943-45)* (Milan: Franco Angeli, 1984), 261, 738n147. Giannantoni's detailed study is the main source for this chapter.

2. Francesco Scomazzon, *"Maledetti figli di Giuda, vi prenderemo!": La caccia nazifascista agli ebrei in una terra di confine, Varese 1943-1945* (Arterigere: Varese, 2005), 60–61.

3. Information report from the Prefect of Sondrio to the Central Public Security Department, December 14, 1943, quoted in Franzinelli, *Delatori*, 181.

4. From the questioning of Police Chief Solinas by the investigating judge, May 8, 1945, cited in Giannantoni, *Fascismo, guerra e società*, 254.

5. Scomazzon, *"Maledetti figli di Giuda,"* 71.

6. From the testimony in the trial of collaborationist guides held in May 1946, see ibid., 114–15; for the figures given, see pp. 83, 108.

7. See Renata Broggini, *Terra d'asilo: I rifugiati italiani in Svizzera 1943-1945* (Bologna: Mulino, 1993), 126–33; these pages—

seven out of a total of 716—are the only ones this study dedicates to those who were refused entry (including Fascists who fled toward the end of the war and even the RSI minister Buffarini Guidi himself).

8. Scomazzon, *"Maledetti figli di Giuda,"* 146n.

9. Ibid., 152.

10. This reconstruction is contained in a letter from Balconi to the police chief of Varese, dated September 20, 1945, cited in Giannantoni, *Fascismo, guerra e società*, 271.

11. Ibid., 746n134.

12. From testimony contained in a letter written in 1982; ibid., 745n179.

13. The reconstruction is by Franzinelli, *Delatori*, 183–86, who publishes the sentences of February 19, 1947 (297–403). See Giannantoni, *Fascismo, guerra e società*, 743–44, 744n169.

14. The report, contained in the State Archive of Como, is quoted in *Rapporto* 2001 of the Anselmi Committee, 91–92. See also Sarfatti, *The Jews in Mussolini's Italy*, 191.

Chapter Eight

1. See "Giudei," *Brescia Repubblicana*, December 1, 1943, cited in Marino Ruzzenenti, *La capitale della Rsi e la Shoah: La persecuzione degli ebrei nel Bresciano (1938-1945)*, Studi Bresciani: Quaderni della Fondazione Micheletti, 16 (Rudiano [Brescia]: GAM, 2006), 73. The reconstructions and quotations in this chapter are taken from this volume, which Ruzzenenti also drew upon for his *Shoah: Le colpe degli italiani* (Rome: Manifestolibri, 2011). On Brescia in the RSI, see also the catalogue for the exhibition *Il Giorno della Memoria 2007: 1938-1945, la persecuzione degli ebrei in Italia e l'antisemitismo a Brescia* (Brescia: Palazzo Martinengo, 2007).

2. Here, as in the chapter title, I transpose the title of the novel *The City without Jews*, a fictional work by the Viennese writer Hugo Bettauer, who already in 1922 imagined the tragic consequences of German and Austrian antisemitism. He was murdered by a Nazi sympathizer in 1925.

3. The Della Volta affair is reconstructed by Ruzzenenti, *La capitale della RSI e la Shoah*, 73–90.

4. Ibid., 117.

5. Ibid., 116.

6. Ibid.

7. Ibid.

8. Ibid., 118.

9. These cases are documented and reconstructed in ibid., 116–19, 122.

10. "Exonerated" Jews were, as previously mentioned, Jewish citizens for whom the anti-Jewish measures had been partly alleviated, usually for patriotic activities.

11. On the denunciation of Lenghi, see Ruzzenenti, *La capitale della RSI e la Shoah*, 122–23; on the Apollonio printworks as the new seat of the state Polygraphic Institute, see pp. 146, 171n2.

12. For the episode, see ibid., 125.

13. The Loewy affair is reconstructed in ibid., 103–6.

Chapter Nine

1. Hannah Arendt, *Eichmann in Jerusalem: A Report on the Banality of Evil* (New York: Viking Press, 1963); Primo Levi, *The Drowned and the Saved*, translated by Raymond Rosenthal and Michael Joseph (Turin: Giulio Einaudi, 1986).

2. Stathis N. Kalyvas, *The Logic of Violence in Civil War* (New York: Cambridge University Press, 2006), 336–40.

3. Teresa Pescatori, statement made at the Venice Police Head-quarters, July 14, 1945, in Archive of the Fondazione Centro Documentazione Ebraica Contemporanea, Milan (here-after ACDEC), Processi ai criminali nazisti, Stralci di pro-cessi, box 1, file "Corte d'Assise di Milan Sessione Speciale," Processo Mauro Grini (1945–46).

4. Extract from the Bulletin of the Information Service of the Committee of National Liberation for Northern Italy (*Bollettino del Servizio di Informazioni del Comitato di Liberazione per l'Alta Italia*), no. 18, March 1, 1945, ACDEC, Processi ai criminali nazisti, Stralci di processi, box 1, file "Corte d'Assise di Milan Sessione Speciale," Processo Mauro Grini (1945–46).

5. Typewritten statement, n.d., ACDEC, Processi ai crimi-nali nazisti, Stralci di processi, box 1, file "Corte d'Assise di Milan Sessione Speciale," Processo Mauro Grini (1945–46).

6. Egon and Walter Sussland to the Jewish Community of Trieste, May 23, 1946, ACDEC, Processi ai criminali na-zisti, Stralci di processi, box 1, file "Corte d'Assise di Milan Sessione Speciale," Processo Mauro Grini (1945–46).

7. Venice, police note no. 610, November 1, 1944, in ACDEC, Comunità ebraiche italiane, box 4, file Venezia. According to this source, Grini told his Venetian hotelier that he be-longed to the "Jewish race" and that he was "now at the or-ders of the Germans as part of his own personal odyssey" but that he was and would "always remain a Jew."

8. Press cutting from *Corriere della Sera*, July 6, 1947, in ACDEC, Processi ai criminali nazisti, Stralci di processi, box 1, file "Corte d'Assise di Milan Sessione Speciale," Processo Mauro Grini (1945–46).

9. See Roberto Curci, *Via San Nicolò 30: Traditori e traditi nella Trieste nazista* (Bologna: Il Mulino, 2015).

10. Cialli Mezzaroma set up six squads specializing in hunting down Jews; see Amedeo Osti Guerrazzi, *"La repubblica necessaria": Il fascismo repubblicano a Roma, 1943-44* (Milan: Franco Angeli, 2004), 62.

11. For the entire matter, see Osti Guerrazzi, *Caino a Roma*, 106–10, and Foa, *Portico d'Ottavia*.

12. The testimonies and denunciations of her fellow Jews were documented not only in the trials held soon after the war but also in the pamphlet *Pantera near: Eri la spia di piazza Giudia* (Rome: Stabilimento tipografico de "Il Giornale d'Italia," 1945).

13. Interview with Gabriella Ajò by Silvia Haia Antonucci, in Archivio Storico della Comunità Ebraica di Rome, *Rome, 16 ottobre 1943: Anatomia di una deportazione* (Milan: Guerini, 2006), 99.

14. Interview with Speranza Ajò, in Archivio Storico della Comunità Ebraica di Rome, *Rome, 16 ottobre 1943*, 106.

15. Interview with Rina Calò, in Archivio Storico della Comunità Ebraica di Rome, *Rome, 16 ottobre 1943*, 111.

16. Interview with Alberto Sed, in Archivio Storico della Comunità Ebraica di Rome, *Rome, 16 ottobre 1943*, 131.

17. Interrogation of Bruno Pastacaldi, August 9, 1946, quoted in Baiardi, "Persecuzioni antiebraiche a Firenze," 121. For his profile, see pp. 117–18.

18. Osti Guerrazzi, *Caino a Roma*, 111–12.

19. Ibid., 91–92.

20. The expressions belong to Baiardi, "Persecuzioni antiebraiche a Firenze," 56.

21. The letter is quoted in the original form with its uncertain grammar, and the matter is reconstructed in *Ultime lettere di condannati a morte e di deportati della Resistenza 1943-1945*, edited by Mimmo Franzinelli (Milan: Mondadori, 2006), 304.

22. These episodes are cited by Mimmo Franzinelli, "Collaborazione e delazione," in *Storia della Shoah in Italia*, edited

by Flores et al., 1:563, from an unpublished diary held in the CDEC archives in Milan, and from a note written by the Roman chief of police to the Directorate General of Public Security, November 15, 1943.

23. Luciano Allegra, *Gli aguzzini di Mimo: Storie di ordinario collaborazionismo (1943-1945)* (Turin: Zamorani, 2010), 97.

24. Ibid., 112.

Conclusion

1. Giacomo Debenedetti, *Otto ebrei* (1944), in *Saggi*, edited by Alfonso Berardinelli (Milan: Mondadori, 1999), 71.

2. Mimmo Franzinelli, *L'amnistia Togliatti: 22 giugno 1946: Colpo di spugna sui crimini fascisti* (Milan: Mondadori, 2006), 55–56.

3. On the theme of sanctions against Fascism and the continuity of the state, see the classic study by Claudio Pavone, *La continuità dello Stato: Istituzioni e uomini* (1974), now in Claudio Pavone, *Alle origini della Repubblica: Scritti su fascismo, antifascismo e continuità dello Stato* (Turin: Bollati Boringhieri, 1995).

4. Franzinelli, *L'amnistia Togliatti*, 15.

5. Ibid., 28, 41–42.

6. Ibid., 170.

7. Ibid., 148, 181.

8. Ibid., 51.

9. Ibid., 49.

10. Regarding these processes, see Filippo Focardi, *Il cattivo tedesco e il bravo italiano: La rimozione delle colpe della seconda guerra mondiale* (Rome: Laterza, 2013).

11. Quoted in ibid., 123.

12. The quotation is taken from "Fascist Rescue of Jews Revealed," *New York Times*, May 22, 1946; see also the groundbreaking work by French historian Léon Poliakov. See also

Guri Schwarz, *After Mussolini: Jewish Life and Jewish Memories in Post-Fascist Italy*, translated by Giovanni Noor Mazhar (Rome, 2005; London: Vallentine Mitchell, 2005), 131–33.

13. Schwarz, *After Mussolini*, 177.

14. Quoted in ibid., 157. On Vitale's activities, see Costantino Di Sante, *Auschwitz prima di "Auschwitz": Massimo Adolfo Vitale e le prime ricerche sugli ebrei deportati dall'Italia* (Verona: Ombrecorte, 2014).

15. Schwartz, *After Mussolini*, 152, for the words by the Italian Jewish leader and the comments made by Schwarz about De Felice.

16. Robert S. C. Gordon, *The Holocaust in Italian Culture, 1944–2010* (Stanford: Stanford University Press, 2012), 150. Gordon also analyzes the role that various Italian films played in this process.

17. David Bidussa, *Il mito del bravo italiano* (Milan: Il Saggiatore, 1994); *Italiani brava gente? Un mito duro a morire*, edited by Angelo Del Boca (Vicenza: Neri Pozza, 2010).

18. See Francesco Germinario, *L'altra memoria: L'estrema destra, Salò e la Resistenza* (Turin: Bollati Boringhieri, 1999), 58–73.

19. See Focardi, *Il cattivo tedesco e il bravo italiano*, 118, 122, 127–28, 130, 240n47, 244n89. Davide Rodogno, *Fascism's European Empire: Italian Occupation during the Second World War* (Cambridge: Cambridge University Press, 2006), offers the most in-depth analysis of the matter, showing how the refusal to hand over the Jews was actually dictated by motives of prestige and the defense of Italian interests and decision-making powers in the Balkans.

20. *I giusti d'Italia: I non ebrei che salvarono gli ebrei 1943–1945*, edited by Israel Gutman, Bracha Rivlin, and Liliana Picciotto (Jerusalem, 2004; Milan: Yad Vashem-Mondadori, 2006); Patricia Cohen, "Italian Praised for Saving Jews Is Now Seen as Nazi Collaborator," *New York Times*, June 19, 2013.

21. Antonio Carioti, "'Palatucci non fu un giusto': Yad Vashem riapre la questione," *Corriere della Sera*, June 23, 2013.
22. This stereotypical image emerges repeatedly in the volume promoted by Yad Vashem, *I giusti d'Italia*, for example, p. xxxvii. For Picciotto's criticisms of the preliminary research see her chapter in ibid., 264.
23. These figures are taken from the official statistics published by Yad Vashem, "Names and Numbers of the Righteous among the Nation per Country and Ethnic Origin as of January 1, 2013," http://www.yadvashem.org/yv/en/righteous/statistics.asp (updated December 2013).
24. Italian Law No. 211 of July 20, 2000, art. 1: "The Italian Republic recognizes January 27, the date of the liberation of Auschwitz, as 'Giorno della Memoria' [Memorial Day], with the aim of recalling the Shoah (the extermination of the Jewish people), the racial laws, the Italian persecution of Jewish citizens, the Italians who were subjected to deportation, imprisonment, and death, as well as all those who, in varying fields of action and with varying political allegiances, saved other lives and protected the persecuted at the risk of their own lives."
25. Baiardi, "Persecuzioni antiebraiche a Firenze," 94.
26. Foa, *Portico d'Ottavia*, 104.
27. On the recasting of Cortellini and the ambiguity of this figure, see Paolo Sereni, "Gli anni delle persecuzioni razziali a Venezia: Appunti per una storia," in *Venezia ebraica: Atti delle prime giornate di studio sull'ebraismo veneziano (Venezia, 1976–1980)*, edited by Umberto Fortis (Rome: Carucci, 1982), 146n. Evidence in favor of Cortellini emerges in the memoirs of Giorgio Soppelsa, *Dal fondo degli anni: Il Novecento di un veneziano di montagna*, Istituto veneziano per la storia della Resistenza della società contemporanea (Venice: La Toletta, 2014), 106–7, but I find this interpretation controversial.

On the "chameleon-like qualities" of the police forces from the RSI period to the Liberation, especially with regard to Venice, see Marco Borghi and Alessandro Reberschegg, *Fascisti alla sbarra: L'attività della Corte d'Assise straordinaria di Venezia, 1945–1947* (Venice: Comune di Venezia-Istituto veneziano per la storia della Resistenza della società contemporanea, 1999), 59.

28. Communication dated July 5, 2013, from Mariapina Di Simone, head of the study room in the Archivio Centrale dello Stato (Rome), whom I would like to thank.

29. Annette Wieviorka, *The Era of the Witness*, translated by Jared Stark (Paris, 1998; Ithaca, NY: Cornell University Press, 2006).

Glossary

badogliani. Literally the followers of General Pietro Badoglio, who was prime minister after the fall of Mussolini in July 1943 for forty-five days. The term was usually used by the Fascists (and by the Germans) to indicate all those Italians who had betrayed or had not remained faithful to Mussolini after his fall and his subsequent return to power in September 1943.

Brigate Nere (Black Brigades). The armed branch of the Fascist party established in June 1944.

carabinieri. The Italian military police.

Carità gang. Officially the Special Services Branch of the 92nd Legion of the MVSN paramilitary. Founded and led by Major Mario Carità, it was a paramilitary squad that practiced *squadrismo* and was notorious for its brutality.

Comitato Ricerche Deportati Ebrei (Research Committee on Jewish Deportees). Established in 1944 by the Union of Italian Jewish Communities, tasked with locating surviving deportees, researching the fates of deceased deportees, and providing information to family members.

Corpo Volontari della Libertà (CVL). The Freedom Volunteer Corps established formally in the summer of 1944 as the official army uniting the various partisan formations fighting in the anti-Fascist Resistance until the Liberation of Italy in April 1945.

Demorazza. Office charged with handling racial affairs within the Italian Ministry of the Interior. Its official title was

Direzione Generale per la Demografia e la Razza (Directorate General for Demography and Race).

Ente Comunale di Assistenza (ECA). The Municipal Assistance Agency, which, during the Italian Social Republic, received confiscated Jewish property officially to be reallocated to Italians in need.

Ente di Gestione e Liquidazione Immobiliare (EGELI). Agency for the Management and Liquidation of [Jewish] Property. It was established in 1939 following the promulgation of the racial laws.

Fascist Party. *See* **Partito Fascista Repubblicano**.

finanzieri. Agents of the Guardia di Finanza.

General Inspectorate of Race. Started in March 1944 and led by Giovanni Preziosi; engaged in racial identification, the dissemination of antisemitic propaganda, and the monthly publication of its review titled *Razza e civiltà* (Race and civilization).

Guardia di Finanza (Finance Guard). A military branch of police responsible for the enforcement of customs, excise, and tax.

Milizia volontaria di sicurezza nazionale (MVSN). The Voluntary Militia for National Security. The paramilitary arm of the Partito Nazionale Fascista (PNF) during Italy's twenty-year Fascist period. In December 1943, during the Italian Social Republic, it was integrated into the National Republican Guard.

National Republican Guard (GNR). Established in December 1943 as the continuation of the MVSN; included members of the Milizia and of the *carabinieri*. It acted as both military and police force for the Italian Social Republic, and in the summer of 1944 it became part of the national Republican Army.

Partito Fascista Repubblicano (PFR). Republican Fascist Party that governed Italy from September 1943 when Mussolini was reinstated to power as the head of the government of the Italian Social Republic until the Liberation and collapse of the Republic in April 1945.

Party, the. *See* **Partito Fascista Repubblicano**.

Repubblica Sociale Italiana (RSI). The Italian Social Republic, also known as the Republic of Salò. It was the state name of Italy and the government led by the PFR, and headed by Benito Mussolini as prime minister, under the influence of the German occupiers. This government ruled central and northern Italy from September 1943 until the Allied Liberation in April 1945.

Republic of Salò. *See* **Repubblica Sociale Italiana**.

squadrismo. The ideologically motivated Fascist violence and actions of the paramilitary squads especially at the origins of Fascism (1919–22). Its style of action and spirit was revived by the Fascist squads (for example, the Carità gang) during the Repubblica Sociale Italiana.

squadrista. A member of a paramilitary Fascist squad that practiced *squadrismo*.

Index

during the Italian genocide by ("Togliatti amnesty" [presidential decree no. 4, June 22, 1946]), 132–33; highlighting of the tolerance and kindheartedness of Italians toward Jews in the international press, 135–36; and the Italian Jewish elite, 136; minimization of the role of the RSI, 138; the Ministry of Foreign Affairs' promotion of the reduction or negation of Italian responsibility in anti-Jewish policies, 135; the "myth of the good Italian," 135; post–World War II stereotypes and mainstream portrayals of, 137–38. See also "Righteous," the

Jarak, Ines, 114
Jewish Affairs Office of the Prefecture of Ferrara, 71
Jewish property, seizure of in Italy, 5, 67–75; bureaucratic procedures for, 67–71; and the EGELI, 68–69, 74; sequestration decrees, 68, 88; true thefts or robberies, 72–73
Jews, and the 1943–45 Italian genocide, 7; the beginning of the persecution, 59–66; "exonerated" Jews, 150n23, 159n3, 168n10; the first deportation transport (December 6, 1943), 50; and Jewish minors, 2, 85, 162n6; the killing of Jews on Italian soil, 56, 57; the main German concentration camps where Jewish deportees were sent, 58; and Nazi roundups of Jews, 32, 49, 60; and the plans for a vast concentration camp system, 48; statistics on arrests, deportations, and murders

on Italian soil, 56–58. See also Brescia, arrests and deportations of Jews from; Florence, arrests and deportations of Jews from; Italians, recasting of the role of in the 1943–45 genocide; Jews, arrests and deportations of those fleeing to seek refuge in Switzerland; Venice, arrests and deportations of Jews from
Jews, arrests and deportations of those fleeing to seek refuge in Switzerland, 101–9; and the betrayal of guides, 102, 104, 105–8; and guide fees, 104; and protection by the finanzieri, 104–5
Jews, in Italy, cities with the largest Jewish populations, 57
"Jews as the Disease of Humanity, The" (Protti), 2, 19, 20
Jews in Fascist Italy, The: A History (De Felice), 137

Kalyvas, Stathis N., 12
Kappler, Herbert, 50
Koch, Pietro, 34–36

La confisca dei beni ebraici (The confiscation of Jewish assets; Martelloni), 18
La finanza ebraica alla conquista dei paesi arabi (The role of Jewish finance in conquering Arab countries), 24
La provincia, 21
La questione giudaica vista dai Cattolici oltre cinquant'anni fa (The Jewish question as seen by Catholics over fifty years ago), 24
La Stampa, 23
La Vita Italiana, 14–15